An Illustrated History of

HULL'S RAILWAYS

M. Nicholson and W.B. Yeadon

PREFACE

This account deals with the rail services we once had, and the lines in the city on which trains still operate. We deliberately ignore the wheeler–dealer activities of the lawyers, financiers, stockbrokers, landowners, promoters, and political gentlemen who concerned themselves with arguing about, and providing the railway network in, and around, Hull. Those interested in such aspects are well catered for in a number of detailed studies by eminent authorities. They can refer to the following:–

A History of Hull Railways, by G.G. Mac-Turk, published in 1879.

The up–dated edition of Macturk published in 1970, which contains research by that acknowledged authority, the late Ken Hoole.

The North Eastern Railway – Its Rise & Development, an 820 page volume by W.W. Tomlinson, published in 1914.

The Hull & Barnsley Railway, Volume 1, published in 1972 by a team of six specialists on that railway, and edited by K. Hoole.

The Hull & Barnsley Railway, Volume 2, published in 1980 by a team of eleven specialists, and edited by B.Hinchcliffe.

Together, those five volumes total 1613 pages, with copious illustrations and maps, so most general aspects are covered, and most railway society libraries have them.

However, when the Act of Parliament has been obtained, the permanent way, bridges, tunnels and stations completed, engines, coaches and wagons built or purchased, all that prodigious effort and expense is of no avail whatever until the 'railwaymen' take up their widely diverse duties. In more than 150 years they established & maintained standards of safety and reliability, of which they can be proud, day and night, winter and summer, 24 hours a day, for 365 (or 366) days every year. The main responsibilities rested with the men who cared for the track, on those who fired and drove the engines, and especially the signalmen, yet very few indeed had been educated beyond elementary school level. So, our account is particularly concerned with those who control and move the trains. In this city, apart from one major lapse in February 1927, they have an almost impeccable record.

IRWELL PRESS ≈≈≈≈≈

Copyright Irwell Press 1993
ISBN 1-871608-44-9
Printed by Amadeus Press, Huddersfield
First published in UK by Irwell Press, 15 Lovers Lane, Grasscroft, OLDHAM OL4 4DP.

INTRODUCTION

The city of Hull is semi–circular in plan, with its base, the three mile wide River Humber, proving an effective barrier to communication with the south. To the east, the Yorkshire coast of the North Sea is only an average of twenty miles away. Thus, Hull perforce had to look to the north and west for inland travel and trade. To the north was only the small ecclesiastical town of Beverley, and after that little in the way of people, until the holiday resorts of Bridlington, 31 miles, and Scarborough, 54 miles away. So Hull inevitably looked to the west as the only likely profitable direction, and had to accept that its situation was indeed 'at the end of the line'. It is still a city to which anyone has to make a deliberate effort to visit, because it is not on the way to anywhere else. Since the start of North Sea Ferries on 17th December 1965 to and from the continent, there is now a constant flow of travellers briefly breathing our air as their cars and lorries pass through, but the great majority of them, simply do 'pass through'. They make a minimal contribution to the city's prosperity, and hardly even see Hull.

Other geographical features needing to be appreciated are that the average height of the city is no more than seven feet above sea level, and that Selby, 31 miles away to the west, is only twelve feet higher; also that the city is bisected by the River Hull – from that river the city takes its official name of Kingston – upon – Hull, but its railways, in timetables, publicity and station nameboards, has followed the common usage of simply Hull, so we are content to do likewise.

THE DEVELOPMENT OF HULL'S RAILWAYS

The first date of significance is July 1st 1840, when the Hull and Selby Railway began operation from Manor House station in Railway Street, just to the west of Humber Dock, to make an end–on junction 31 miles westward with the Leeds and Selby Railway. It had no steeper gradient than 1 in 572, and one stretch of 18 miles was (and is) straight. It is still Hull's main line, and we shall deal with it in detail later as far out as Hessle Haven. From July 1st 1845 the Hull and Selby was leased to George Hudson's York and North Midland Railway. That latter railway next established a branch from Hull to Bridlington, which became operative from October 6th 1846. It left the Selby line just over a mile out of Manor House station, and by the time Bridlington was reached, it had traversed 37 level crossings, appreciably more than one for every mile, and some of them may even yet be factors in the closure of the line. On it, Cottingham South junction is our outward limit for description of the Bridlington line.

The York and North Midland completed the link between Scarborough and Bridlington for operation from October 20th 1847, so in just over seven years, Hull had obtained both its westward and northward rail connections. Its traffic growth quickly out–grew what Manor House station could cope with – not at all surprising considering there were only single arrival and departure platforms. At first, trains stopped outside, the engine was detached, and the carriages were hauled into the platform by a rope! The York and North Midland soon

decided that it would be to their advantage to have the necessarily bigger station nearer to the centre of the city, so 4½ miles of new lines were laid. Those from Hessle Junction converged with those from Cottingham Junction at West Parade Junction, half a mile from the magnificent station and hotel which G.T. Andrews designed at the end of Paragon Street, although the station's main entrance was on Anlaby Road. Its original name of Paragon Street underwent contraction to just Paragon, and now it is simply Hull station. With Paragon's opening on May 8th 1848, Manor House station closed to passengers, and retained only as a goods station.

The hotel was completed in 1849 but did not open for patrons until 1851. Following an overnight stay on 13/14th October 1854, Queen Victoria gave permission for it to be named the Royal Station Hotel. Along with Prince Albert, and five of their children, they left from Corporation Pier in the Royal yacht *FAIRY* to visit Grimsby. Successively owned by the York and North Midland, the North Eastern, the London & North Eastern, and the Hotels Executive of British Railways, the hotel was finally sold out of railway ownership in 1983. It was enlarged twice, in 1909 and 1935. Sadly, the new owners of this Grade II listed building have dropped 'Station' from its name, all

Paragon station 29th September 1959 with a Hull – Liverpool train departing behind V2 No.60863. The Leicester based engine was on a running–in turn, after a recent overhaul at Doncaster, and will take its train as far as Leeds. The services to Liverpool via Manchester are still prominent in today's timetable. photograph Ken Hoole.

the more regrettable when you have an excellent view of the platforms and the circulating area whilst enjoying excellent fare in its restaurant. In Hull today, if you ask to be directed to the Royal Hotel (its current name), there is an even chance that you will be sent to the public house in New Bridge Road, but ask for the Station Hotel and you will have no difficulty.

LOCAL BRANCHES

From October 20th 1847 Hull had rail connection to the north with Scarborough, and to the west with Selby, on lines which are still operative. Until then, all activity had been on the west side of the river Hull, where the docks which were then open were also located. The conversion of Manor House station to handling only goods enabled it to deal quite adequately with the traffic from the four small docks – Queen's, Prince's, Humber & Railway respectively. However the next dock to open, Victoria, in 1850, (as well as an extension to it in 1852) was on the eastern side of the river Hull, posing the inevitable question of bridging it – the only way rail traffic could be secured from the new dock. The York and North Midland recognised that such traffic would be important, and on May 16th 1853 accordingly opened a line to it. Starting from Anlaby Road Junction on the Selby line, at a point almost a mile out of Paragon station, it crossed the Bridlington line on the flat, and then ran round the outskirts of the city to terminate at Victoria Dock station, adjacent to the north side of the new dock. To enable it to cross the river Hull an opening bridge had to be provided, allowing ships as far upstream as Beverley. So a swing bridge was constructed at Sculcoates. It was envisaged that the new line might generate some suburban passenger traffic, so Manor House was reopened to passengers, and new stations were provided at Stepney (with a level crossing of Beverley Road), at Sculcoates (where the line crossed Stoneferry Road), and at Southcoates on Holderness Road, which had linked that district with Hull since 1305. The Victoria Dock line crossed what is now known as Wincolmlee directly east of the original Sculcoates station. Stoneferry Road, now called Clevland Street, was also crossed on the level, and at that time the first Wilmington station, which lay just to the east, was still in use. Victoria Dock station, moreover, was sited on the south side of the road to Hedon, involving yet another level crossing of a main road. The expected suburban traffic never materialised, even after it was based upon Paragon instead of Manor House, so it ceased to operate from November 1st 1854. However, goods traffic was such that, for more than a hundred years, the frequent closing of its level crossings caused irritation and delay to road users. In 1864 the Victoria Dock branch was doubled and then carried a prodigious amount of imports, mainly of Scandinavian and Baltic timber, which had to be tripped to the Outwards Yard at Dairycoates (on the west side of the city) where it could join main line goods trains.

Promoted by landowners in the district, and local dignitaries, an independent company launched the Hull and Holderness Railway, to connect Hull with Hedon and the seaside town of Withernsea. Opened on June 27th 1854, it was allowed by the York and North Midland to use Victoria Dock station as its Hull terminus. Actually, this new line had been granted running powers (which it never sought to exercise) into Paragon Street station by an agreement made in 1853.

Though anticipating events, here it is convenient to mention that from January 1st 1860, the North Eastern Railway took over the working of the Hull and Holderness and then, under an Act dated July 7th 1862, absorbed it. Along with the 1864 doubling of the Victoria Dock branch, a ¼ mile curve was put in east of Southcoates station, enabling Withernsea trains to run direct to and from Paragon Street, which they did from June 1st 1864. The station on Victoria Dock was closed to passengers. When it was pulled down about 1980 to make way for road improvements the station house and its typical booking office window disappeared at last.

Hull's railway horizon widened tremendously from July 31st 1854 when the North Eastern Railway came into existence, through the amalgamation of the York and North Midland, the York, Newcastle and Berwick, and the Leeds Northern Railways. That put 720 miles of railway, and a capital of £23 millions under the same ownership, a very powerful combination indeed.

East of Hull there could only be potential traffic from agriculture, and from seaside visitors, but that did not deter the promotion of the Hull and Hornsea Railway, an independent Company, which opened the 13 mile line from Hornsea to a junction with the North Eastern's Victoria Dock branch at Wilmington on March 28th 1864. But it was worked by the North Eastern from the start, and the line's independence was brief, the North Eastern taking it over completely from July 16th 1866. When opened, trains ran only to and from Wilmington, the intended through running to and from Paragon Street station being delayed until July 1st 1864, because the initial arrangement of the junction did not satisfy the Board of Trade's Inspector.

With the opening of the Victoria Dock branch in 1853, the new 1848 lines of the Bridlington branch diversion were crossed on the level. Unlike in other countries – most notably America – flat crossings were not a common feature of British operating practice. In all there were little more than half a dozen examples in the land, and coincidentally more than one was on the NER. From the earliest days signalling of some sort must have existed here, and this is further reflected by the railway cottage on the left, no doubt provided to accommodate the early signalman and his family. A signal box and signalling much as we know it today was in use here by 1877. At first this controlled only the flat crossing, which like the signal box itself was appropriately known as Victoria Crossing. During 1891 a trailing mains crossover, and a facing connection to the new Walton Street carriage sidings, was provided. The signal box was situated just behind the engine on the down side of the Bridlington line, and it finally closed at 8.00 a.m. on 8th July 1945. After this the nearby West Parade signal box assumed control of all the existing points and signals. These alterations, which had first been estimated to cost £3,131, had reached the committee stage as long ago as 27th July 1939 only to be held back by the war. After regular passenger traffic ceased in 1854 the short portion of the Victoria Dock branch between Anlaby Road and Botanic Gardens Junctions (1,143 yards) nominally became goods only. Even so, in order to avoid reversal at Paragon (a similar situation existed between Hessle Road and Cottingham South Junctions) summer excursions from the West Riding used this route to gain direct access to the Hornsea and Withernsea branches. This came to an end in 1964 when the passenger service was withdrawn from both lines and only a rapidly dwindling goods traffic continued to use the line. This ceased on 28th October 1968, when the Victoria Dock branch west of Wilmington Junction was officially closed. Carrying class 'A' headlamps, a York B16/1 4–6–0 No.61452 negotiates the crossing in the late 1950's.

3

THE DIRECT LINKS TO YORK AND TO DONCASTER

Although powers had been granted on June 18th 1846 for a line between Beverley and York, only the portion from York to Market Weighton was constructed under them, and that line was opened on October 4th 1847. It was not until May 1st 1865 that the North Eastern linked Hull directly with York by opening the Beverley to Market Weighton section.

Another, similar, link of great importance to Hull was the opening on July 30th 1869 of the line from Staddlethorpe, 17 miles out of the city on the Hull – Selby line, to Thorne junction on the Manchester, Sheffield and Lincolnshire's line from Doncaster to Grimsby, which cut 9 miles from the Hull to London journey. As part of the deal to build that new line, the North Eastern granted running powers into Hull to the Lancashire and Yorkshire and to the Manchester, Sheffield and Lincolnshire (Great Central from August 1st 1897) Railways. This resulted in Hull gaining three regular services, by different routes, to Manchester and Liverpool.

The running powers into Hull obtained by the Manchester, Sheffield and Lincolnshire Railway were a useful supplement to the access that the Company had possessed since March 1st 1849. Their railway extended to the end of a 1,500 foot long pier out into the river Humber at New Holland, from which steam–driven paddle ships maintained a regular ferry service across to Hull. During some low tides, passengers at the Hull end had to resort to small boats to leave, or join, the ferry boat, but that inconvenience was overcome in 1856 by the Railway making an annual payment of £40 to the Mayor and Corporation of Hull for use of the landing facilities at Victoria Pier, which was owned by the Corporation. In 1849 the Manchester, Sheffield and Lincolnshire Railway purchased No.7 Nelson Street, immediately opposite Hull's Victoria Pier entrance, for use as a booking office for passengers and parcels on its ferry boats; in effect, a railway station, but one which a train never reached. Those premises were enlarged in 1854, and again in 1880, when a substantial brick building was erected, which had all the usual offices and facilities

of a railway station. Although closed when the Humber Road Bridge opened in 1981, that station building still exists and displays the *M S L* initials and *1880* in a trefoil device below the roof. In L N E R and also in British Railways timetables, Hull (Corporation Pier) continued to be shown in the *Index to Stations* until the ferry service ceased in July 1981 on the opening of the Humber Bridge to road traffic.

FINAL MAJOR DEVELOPMENT

The final significant addition to Hull's Railways was the opening on July 27th 1885 of the Hull, Barnsley & West Riding Junction Railway & Dock Co. It certainly reached the West Riding of Yorkshire, but the nearest it got to Barnsley was 2¾ miles away, where it joined the Midland Railway at Monk Bretton Junction, and at Stairfoot, which was 2 miles away, where it connected with the Manchester, Sheffield & Lincolnshire, as then named. For passengers, the effective western end of the line was the joint station with the Midland Railway at Cudworth. By changing there into Midland main line trains, they could go on to Sheffield; however from July 1st 1905 running powers were granted enabling the Hull and Barnsley to operate through trains from Hull to Sheffield. The H & B needed new, and better carriages for that service, and so it was not until October 2nd 1905 that it began to operate the through trains. Due to the stringencies of the 1914–18 war these through Sheffield trains were cut back to Cudworth, and never restored subsequently.

So, except for the Hull and Barnsley (which was never considered significant for passenger traffic, other than local and short journey) by the end of 1869, Hull had adequate passenger services on the lines to Doncaster, Leeds, Scarborough, York, Hornsea, and Withernsea. Here are the departures which Paragon Station provided:

NORTH EASTERN RAILWAY PASSENGER DEPARTURES FROM HULL PARAGON ON JUNE 1ST 1870

a.m.
5.50 stopping train to Leeds
6.00 stopping train to Doncaster
6.30 stopping train to Scarborough
6.35 stopping train to York
7.00 stopping train to Hornsea
7.05 fast train to Doncaster
7.05 stopping train to Withernsea
7.35 semi–fast to Withernsea
8.05 Hessle, Ferriby, & Brough
8.15 semi–fast to Hornsea
8.35 semi–fast to Leeds
9.20 stopping train to York
9.25 fast to Normanton & to Leeds
10.00 fast train to Doncaster
10.00 stopping train to Withernsea
10.05 stopping train to Hornsea
10.10 semi–fast to Scarborough
10.40 semi–fast to Leeds
11.35 stopping train to Doncaster
p.m.
12.35 stopping train to Scarborough
1.15 semi–fast to York
2.15 stopping train to Withernsea
2.20 stopping train to Leeds
2.30 stopping train to Hornsea
3.25 fast train to Leeds
3.30 Cottingham & Beverley
3.45 stopping train to Selby
4.00 fast train to Doncaster

The MS&LR originated the Humber ferry crossing from New Holland. This fine looking station was provided by them at the Hull Pier in 1880. Although never rail connected it remained in use until made redundant by the Humber Bridge. Photograph I.K. Watson.

4.00 fast train to Hornsea
4.30 Hessle, Ferriby, & Brough
4.40 stopping train to York
4.45 stopping train to Withernsea
4.55 semi–fast to Scarborough
5.00 fast train to Doncaster
5.15 fast train to Leeds
5.40 semi–fast to Hornsea
5.45 stopping train to Leeds
5.50 fast train to Withernsea
6.00 stopping train to Scarborough
6.30 stopping train to Doncaster
8.00 semi–fast to Leeds
8.05 stopping train to Hornsea
8.30 stopping train to Driffield
8.50 mail train to Leeds

HULL'S OWN RAILWAY

The Hull and Barnsley was not envisaged as a passenger line. It came into being to haul coal from West Riding pits to its Alexandra Dock for export, the return wagons conveniently earning further revenue by taking imported pit props back to the collieries. Until the 1914–18 war however there was also a considerable traffic from the Fish Dock, and in imports of meat, butter, eggs, and fruit. There are few aware, even amongst railway enthusiasts, that each Monday morning between 2.30 and 5.40 a.m. three 'Express Butter' trains were run from Neptune Street goods depot, or that, in 1906 the Hull and Barnsley handled 4,000 tons of imported eggs (in short, about 70 million) and egg traffic was then growing steadily! From Alexandra Dock too, a 'Fast Meat' train left regularly at 5.45 p.m. carrying imported frozen meat.

Sponsored by Hull Corporation to break the North Eastern Railway's monopoly, the Hull and Barnsley had a chequered career, finally being absorbed from March 31st 1922 into the rival North Eastern, which itself lost its separate identity in the Grouping effective on January 1st 1923. The detailed history of the Hull and Barnsley makes fascinating reading, and is fully documented in the two volumes written by dedicated researchers and published in 1972 and 1980 respectively. The lines that it added to Hull's Railways, from west to east, were – the extensive sidings around Springhead works and shed, three miles of line to its Dairycoates and Neptune Street goods depots and four miles mostly on embankment, around the outskirts of the city to those it laid around Alexandra Dock. This crossed the river Hull by a high level girder swing bridge; it was devoid of any crossing of roads on the level, which proved a tremendous boon 80 years later. The H&B crossing of the River Hull was always by means of a swing bridge – although the H&B didn't cross any public roads in Hull on the level, it is not generally realised that the largest level crossing on the railway was actually on the Alexandra

Dock. From these lines there were sidings off to National Radiator Co.'s works, to the National Wool Sheds, to Ella Street Coal Depot, to Sculcoates Goods, to British Gas Light Co., to British Extracting Co. & to Burleigh Street Goods, as well as the one mile branch from Beverley Road Junction to Cannon Street passenger and goods station. The passenger station there was an early casualty of the Grouping, for by July 1924 the LNER had put in a 28 chain spur line connection Springhead Junction to Walton Street Junction on the Hull – Beverley line, enabling the Hull – Cudworth passenger trains to be diverted into Paragon station, and Cannon Street to be closed to passengers after the last train arrived from Cudworth on Sunday July 13th 1924, at 5.50 p.m. Earlier in the day it had left Cannon Street as the 'last train' out at 10.30 that morning. That particular service is an outstanding example of the importance of doing dedicated research if reliable dates are to be established, because there are no less than three published photographs all claiming to show Cannon Street's 'last train' and all different!

The first bogus picture appears in *The LNER Magazine* for August 1924 and one would confidently think that this would be the authentic version. Not so, investigation revealing it to be the 5.40 p.m. from Cannon Street to North Cave on Saturday, July 12th, and the single headlamp confirms it was a local stopping train. Because the line ran due north out of the station, the light on the left hand side of engine 2427 shows the sun to be about in the south west, adding proof of an afternoon photograph. Subsequently it was revealed that the man commissioned to take the 'last train' either could not, or would not, turn out on the Sunday morning for the real subject. To obtain the genuine picture the District Superintendent at Dairycoates shed requested his shed clerk to go to Cannon Street on the Sunday morning, July 13th, and photograph the 10.30 a.m. departure, which had engine 2426. His picture shows the right hand side of the engine, with the sun on the eastern side of the line. The second bogus picture appeared in the *Eastern Morning News* (a then local newspaper) and for their news item the photographer went to Cannon Street on the afternoon of Monday July 14th. The picture that he got has some specious claim to be the 'last train' because it is of engine 2429 clearing empty carriages out of the closed station. So you have three out of the five 4–4–0 engines which the H & B possessed, all with painting differences, on three different dates, and all laying claim to the 'last train'. What better example can you have of the 3–card trick of 'spotting the lady'? Cannon Street, as far as passengers were concerned, clearly had to go when Group-

ing took place, but as a consequence, for the first time, H & B trains added to Hull's level crossing problem when they were switched to using Walton Street crossing on Springbank West. Cannon Street continued to be used as a goods station, and a great deal of soft fruit was dealt with there. For example, on July 1st 1924, it handled no less than 17,345 packages of strawberries, and as they arrived, sales took place on the platform. Goods traffic was still dealt with there until it was closed on June 3rd 1968.

Apart from a couple of short connecting lines added later, the last to be added were those associated with the opening on June 26th 1914 of King George Dock, a project undertaken jointly by the North Eastern and the Hull and Barnsley Railways, and the concurrent erection of an oil importing jetty out into the Humber at Saltend. Considerable coal exports went through both Alexandra and King George docks but ultimately the wheel has turned full circle, and on King George dock in 1992, lines had been laid in to what is named Kingston Terminal, for the *importing* of power station coal, and already more than half a million tons have been dealt with there. The facilities at both docks were designed for exporting coal, and it seems ironic to point out that, exactly a hundred years ago, due to a coal strike, almost 200,000 tons were actually imported through Alexandra Dock. It is equally rueful to mention that coal *exports* through Hull in 1913 were 4½ million tons.

FURTHER ADDITION

Using mainly existing goods lines for access, on May 11th 1907 Hull gained another passenger station, at the end of a new line, a mile in length, from a junction at Dairycoates to the new Riverside Quay. This was 2,500 feet long, and varied in width from 85 to 150 feet, but its 16 feet minimum depth of water enabled steamers to berth at all states of the tide. In consequence, regular sailings to and from Zeebrugge jointly between North Eastern, and the Lancashire and Yorkshire Railways began, and boat train connections reached the Quay from as far as Liverpool, and locally from Paragon station.

DECLINE

To this stage, our description has been almost entirely of additions, those to King George Dock, and to Saltend, bringing Hull's railways to their maximum extent less that six weeks before the outbreak of World War 1 on August 4th 1914, a conflict which had a catastrophic effect on the trade through the port, and on the city itself. Since then, despite some recovery in the middle and later 1930s, the chronicle is almost entirely of contractions and line closures. The Railways Act 1921 which made Grouping effective from January 1st 1923 started the slide, with Hull proving that two into one would go. The two Hull railways were to become part of the London & North Eastern Railway, and as a preliminary step the Hull and Barnsley and the North Eastern Railways amalgamated, as mentioned earlier, as from April 1st the previous year. That did not immediately affect any lines, but when the North Eastern looked at the Hull and Barnsley locomotive stock, they withdrew 42 of the 181 engines before the end of 1922, replacing them from their own stock. The next step came on Sunday 13th July 1924, after the last passenger train arrived back at Cannon Street, when Beverley Road station closed completely, and Cannon Street ceased to cater for passengers. (The one mile branch however continued to serve for goods until June 3rd 1968, and it is interesting to note that the gates to the yard still display their H & B roundel.) The status quo was maintained for a few years, until January 1st 1932, when passenger traffic beyond Howden to Cudworth ceased, but that barely affected the Hull railway position at all.

A line entirely within Hull was the next to lose its passenger service, when on September 19th 1938 Riverside Quay station closed at the end of that summer season. It marked the end of the railway–owned steamers which had linked Hull with Continental ports since 1900, but we still had the paddlers TATTERSHALL CASTLE and WINGFIELD CASTLE, built in 1934 and augmented in 1940 by the larger LINCOLN CASTLE, shuttling on the LNER ferry service to and from New Holland, for the rail connections there. So, at the start of the fateful year 1939, Hull's railways were much the same as for the previous 25 years, and we are able to show the official state of activity normal to Paragon station in May 1939, for comparison with the departures it had in 1870...

Arrivals at and Departures of Trains from the PARAGON STATION, and how dealt with
MONDAYS TO FRIDAYS INCLUSIVE

FROM		Arr.	Platform	Dep.	TO	Set Working	Engine Working	Remarks
		a.m.		a.m.				
Hornsea WFO		12 59	2	—	Drawn	C Set	Shed	*Commences 31st May
Withernsea W.F.O.		*1 12*	*3*	—	*North Sidings*	*5.40 a.m. Leeds W.F.O.*	*Shed*	**Commences 31st May*
Doncaster, M.X.		1 45	2	—	No. 14 Platform	7†30 a.m. Doncaster	Dairycoates	
Hull Goods, M.X.		*2 25*	*Yard*	—		*4.0 a.m. Hull Goods*		*Stone Pilot*
Hull Goods, M.O.		*3 25*	*Yard*	—		*5.0 a.m. Hull Goods*		*Stone Pilot*
			Yard	*4 0*	*Hull Goods, M.X.*	*2.25 a.m. Hull Goods*		
Pontefract		4 15	3	—	Walton Street	8.40 p.m. Pontefract	Shed for 7.5 a.m. Selby	
Leeds		4 35	2	—	Stands	7.5 a.m. Leeds	Shed for 7.0 a.m. [Brough	
			Yard	*5 0*	*Hull Goods, M.O.*	*3.25 a.m. Hull Goods*		
Doncaster		5 17	8	—	Drawn	9.30 a.m. Doncaster	Shed	
Shed	S	—	3	5 35	Withernsea	...	R.L.S.	
North Sidings		—	1	5 38	Bridlington	Spare C Set	Shed	
North Sidings		—	9	5 40	Leeds	11.10 p.m. Beverley	Shed	Top End
Shed		—	4	5†41	Beverley	...	Diesel	†Conveys Mails
Walton Street		—	6	5 44	Withernsea	8.52 a.m. Beverley	Shed	
North Sidings		—	1	5 50	Scarborough	10.52 p.m. Beverley	Shed	
Walton Street		—	5	5 58	Sheffield, Victoria	10.31 p.m. Doncaster	Shed	
Shed		—	4	6 15	Beverley	...	R.L.S.	
Shed		—	6	6*20	Hornsea	...	R.L.S.	*Steam train M.O., commencing 29th May
South Sidings		—	5	6 23	South Howden	7.40 p.m. Brough	Pilot	
Beverley		6 26	1	—	Stands	6.45 a.m. Beverley	Diesel	
North Sidings		—	Sdgs.	6†30	Withernsea T.ThO*	10.0 p.m. Scarborough	Shed	*Daily from 30th May
Sidings		—	—	*6†40**	*Riverside Quay M.O.*	*B.C.L.*	*Shed*	**Commences 19th June*
South Sidings		—	6	6 44	Goole	7.25 p.m. Hornsea	Pilot from 5.0 a.m.	
Stands		—	1	6 45	Beverley	6.26 a.m. Beverley	Diesel	
Dairycoates Shed		—	—	*6 50 L.E.*	*Withernsea*	*Light Engine M.W.F.O.*	*Shed*	
South Sidings		—	7	6 50	Brough	Spare Set	Shed	
South Sidings		—	5	6 50	Hornsea	11†5 p.m. Leeds T.Th.O. 8.22 p.m. Brough Ety. W.F.O.	Shed	
Beverley		6 54	5	—	Stands	7.37 a.m. Willerby	R.L.S.	
North Sidings		—	4	7 0	Brough	Spare Set	Shed	
Stands		—	2	7 5	Leeds	4.35 a.m. Leeds	Shed	
Withernsea	S	7 11	5	—	Shed	...	R.L.S.	
North Sidings		—	3	7 10	Arram	7.57 p.m. York	Shed	Workmen's train
Walton Street		—	1	7 15	York	6.30 p.m. Beverley	Shed	
Dairycoates Shed		—	—	*7 20 L.E.*	*Hornsea M.W.F.O.*	*Light Engine*	*Shed*	
Bridlington		7 21	7		Stands	8.5 a.m. Leeds	Shed for 9.3 a.m. Scarborough	
South Sidings		-	6	7 30	Sheffield (Vic.)	1.45 a.m. Doncaster 7.30 p.m. Brough (2 Sets)	Shed	
Stands		—	5	7 37	Willerby	6.54 a.m. Beverley	R.L.S.	
North Sidings		—	3	7 40	Withernsea	11.15 p.m. Withernsea	Pilot	
Withernsea		7 41	5	—	Stands	7.50 a.m. Hornsea	8.15 a.m. Brough	
Leeds		7 43	3	—	Stands	8.0 a.m. Bridlington	Shed for 9.0am Leeds	
North Sidings		—	4	7 45	Beverley	11.24 p.m. Brough	Shed and platform own train	
Beverley		7 46	1	—	Stands	8.10 a.m. Beverley	R.L.S.	
Brough		7†47	4	—	Stands	8.15 a.m. Brough	8.5 a.m. Leeds	
Hornsea		7*48	2	—	No. 4	8.25 a.m. Goole	R.L.S.	*Steam Train M.O. from 29th May
Stands		—	5	7 50	Hornsea	7.41 a.m. Withernsea	Shed	
R.S.Q.M.O.		*7*57*	*6*	—	*Sidings*	*B.C.L.*	...	**Commences 19th June*
Stands		—	3	8 0	Bridlington	7.43 a.m. Leeds	Shed	
Stands...		--	7	8 5	Leeds	7.21 a.m. Bridlington	7.47 a.m. Brough	
Doncaster		8 4	6	—	South Sidings	2.0 p.m. Sheffield	Shed for 10.35 a.m. Sheffield	
Brough		8†8	—	—	Dairycoates Section	4.25 p.m. Brough Etys	Dairycoates	
Stands		—	1	8 10	Beverley	7.46 a.m. Beverley	Diesel	
Arram		8 11	2	—	Stands	8.25 a.m. York	8.55* Sheffield	
Stands			4	8 15	Brough	†7.47 a.m. Brough	7.41 a.m. Withernsea	
Willerby		8 16	1	—	No. 7	8.45 a.m. Brough	R.L.S.	
No. 2		—	4	8 25	Goole‡	7.48 a.m. Hornsea	R.L.S.	From Shed M.O.
Stands		—	2	8 25	York	8.11 a.m. Arram	Shed	[‡Trailer attached
Bridlington		8 31	4	—	North Sidings	12.45 p.m. Beverley		
Hornsea		8 38	2	—	North Sidings	1.15 p.m. Scarborough	9.55 South Howden	
Bridlington		8 42	3	—	Middle Sidings	10.35 a.m. Sheffield	Pilot 8.50 to 10.10, then to Shed	
Goole		8 43	6	—	North Sidings	3.38 p.m. Withernsea*	Pilot to 10.15 a.m.	*1.50 p.m. Hornsea from 29th May
Withernsea		8 44	1	—	Stands	9.3 a.m. Scarborough	Pilot to 1.15 p.m.	
No. 1		—	7	8 45	Brough	8.16 a.m. Willerby	R.L.S.	
South Howden		8 48	4	—	South Sidings	2†0 p.m. Doncaster	Pilot	
Stands	S	—	1	8 48	Scarboro' Q. Relief	8.38 a.m. Hornsea	Shed. Dairycoates	
Beverley		8 52	4	—	North Sidings	5.44 a.m. Withernsea* 4.40 p.m. Brough	... Shed	*4.50 p.m. Hornsea from 29th May
Walton Street		[illegible]	3	8 [illegible]	Manchester and Liverpool	[illegible] 8.56 p.m. Manchester	[illegible] 7.40	
Withernsea		8 56	2	—	Walton Street	5.25 p.m. Withernsea	Pilot	
Bridlington		8 59	3	—	Walton Street	5.30 p.m. Bridlington	Shed	
Walton Street		—	8	9 0	Liverpool, L.M.S.	7.43 p.m. Liverpool	Shed after arrival 7.43 a.m. ex Leeds	FL attached to rear T.O.
Stands		—	1	9 3	Scarborough	8.44 a.m. Withernsea	Shed	
Hornsea		9 5	5	—	Walton Street	5.35 p.m. Beverley 1.20 p.m. Hornsea Th.O.	9.48 a.m. Hornsea	
Brough		9 8	8	—	Walton Street	1.8 p.m. WithernseaT.T.O. 4.40 p.m. Brough	Pilot to 11.30 a.m.	
Arram		9 11	1	—	Stands	9.45 a.m. Beverley	Diesel	
Walton Street		-	7	9 15	Liverpool, L.M.S.	5.15 p.m. Liverpool	Dairycoates	
Leeds via Wetherby		9*21	7	—	Stands	9.50 a.m. Leeds 12.5 p.m. Withernsea	Shed for 11.0 a.m. Leeds	*Two Sets
York		9 24	3	—	Stands	9.55 a.m. South Howden	Shed	
Stands	S	—	5	9 25	*Withernsea	9.5 a.m. Hornsea	Dairycoates	*Runs 23rd July to [20th August
Sidings		—	10	9 25	Pontefract	8.40 p.m. Selby	Shed	
Hornsea		9 28	4	—	Stands	10.10 a.m. Withernsea	Shed	
Stands		—	9	9 30	King's Cross	9.48 p.m. King's Cross and 11.15 p.m. King's Cross	Pilot	
Stands	S	—	2	9 30	Beverley	9.11 a.m. Arram	R.L.S.	
Stands	S	—	*4*	*9 33*	*Hornsea Q. Rlf. M.Th.O.*	*9.16 a.m. Hornsea*	*Shed*	
Withernsea		9 34	2	—	Stands	9.48 a.m. Hornsea	Shed	
North Sidings	S	—	2	9 35	Scarboro' Q. Relief	C Set	Shed	From 1st August to [30th August
Brough		9 36	6	—	Stands	10.15 a.m. Brough	R.L.S.	
Scarborough		9 38	5	—	Drawn	5.8 p.m. Scarborough	Shed	
Stands	S	—	8	9 40	Withernsea	9.8 a.m. Brough	8.52 a.m. Beverley	
Doncaster M.O.	S	9*40	13	—	...	...	Shed	*Not after 22nd Aug.
Stands		—	1	9 45	Beverley	9.11 a.m. Beverley	Diesel	
Stands	S	—	1	9 45	Scarborough	8.56 a.m. Withernsea	Shed	
Leeds		9 49	8	—	No. 6	11.0 a.m. Leeds	Shed for 2.5 p.m. Leeds	
Stands		--	2	9 48	Hornsea	9.34 a.m. Withernsea	Dairycoates	

Arrivals at and Departures of Trains from the PARAGON STATION, and how dealt with—*continued*
MONDAYS TO FRIDAYS INCLUSIVE

FROM		Arr.	Platform	Dep.	TO	Set Working	Engine Working	Remarks
		a.m.		a.m.				
Stands		—	7	9 50	Leeds, via Wetherby	9.21 a.m. Leeds	Pilot 6.0 a.m. to 9.15	
Stands		—	3	9 55	South Howden	9.24 a.m. York	8.38 Hornsea	
Stands	S	—	*5*	*10*0*	*Withernsea Q. Rlf.*	...	*Shed*	**Runs 1st to 31st Aug.*
Sheffield		10 8	7	—	Stands	11.55 a.m. Doncaster	Shed for 11.30 a.m. Doncaster	
Bridlington		10 8	3	—	Stands	11.5 a.m. Scarborough	Shed	
Stands		-	4	10 10	Withernsea	9.28 a.m. Hornsea	Pilot T.Tho.	
Stands		—	6	10 15	Brough	9.36 a.m. Brough	R.L.S.	
Beverley		10 31	4	—	Shed	12.45 p.m. Brough	Diesel	
Middle Sidings		—	9	10 35	Sheffield and Swansea	8.42 a.m. Bridlington 4.45 p.m. Swansea	Shed after 8.4 a.m. Doncaster	[Sept.
Sidings	S	—	3	10 35	Scarborough Q. Rlf.	Made up Set	Shed	Runs 2nd Aug. to 13th
Walton Street	S	—	1	10*43	Withernsea	6.15 p.m. Beverley	Shed. Dairycoates	*Not after 10th Sept.
Billingsgate		10 40	Yard	—	...	Fish Pilot		
Stands		—	*2*	*10*40*	*Scarboro'*	*9.8 p.m. Scarborough*	*Shed*	**Commences 29th May*
Stands	S	—	5	10*50	Hornsea	9.41 Hornsea	Pilot	*Not after 10th Sept.
Leeds		10 54	8	—	Stands	1.0 p.m. Leeds	Shed for 12.1 p.m. York	
No. 8		-	6	11 0	Leeds	9.49 a.m. Leeds	Shed after arrival 9.21 a.m. from Leeds	
York		11 2	2	—	No. 6	12.1 p.m. York	Dairycoates	
Stands		-	3	11 5	Scarborough	10.8 a.m. Bridlington	Shed.	
Brough		11 6	5	—	Shed	12.24 p.m. Beverley	R.L.S.	
South Sidings		—	—	*11†15**	*R.S.Q. ThO*	*B.C.L.*	*Shed*	**Commences 22nd June*
Hornsea		11 20	3	—	Stands	12.8 p.m. Beverley	Shed	And 12.30 p.m. Billingsgate E. and Van
Goole		11 20	4	—	Shed	12.15 p.m. Brough	R.L.S.	Detach trailer
Withernsea*	S	11 24	1	—	Drawn	12.15 p.m. Brough	Shed	*Runs 23rd July to 20th August
		—	10	11 30	King's Cross	8.13 p.m. King's Cross	Shed	Pullman
Scarborough		11 33	5	—	Stands	12.10 p.m. Withernsea	12.8 p.m. Beverley	
Hornsea M.ThO. Q.Ety	S	11 35	Sdgs.	—	Walton Street	1.20 p.m. Hornsea Th.O.	Shed	
Stands	S	—	3	11 40	Withernsea	11.20 a.m. Hornsea	Shed	
Withernsea	S	11 41	2	—	Stands	12.5 p.m. Hornsea	Shed [Selby	
Pontefract		11 45	4	—	No. 10	12.30 p.m. Selby	Shed for 12.30 p.m.	
No. 13		—	9	11 45	Doncaster and King's Cross	5.23 p.m. King's Cross and 10.35 p.m. York	Dairycoates	
South Howden		11 49	2	—	Drawn	4.0 p.m. York	Shed	
Stands		—	7	11 55	Doncaster	10.8 a.m. Sheffield	Shed	
Billingsgate Fish		12 0	F Line	—				
		p.m.		p.m.				
No. 2		--	6	12 1	York	11.2 a.m. York	Shed after arr. 10.54 a.m. from Leeds	
North Sidings		—	1	12 5	Hornsea	9†21 a.m. Leeds	Shed [Sheffield	
Sheffield		12 5	4	—	Stands	1.5 p.m. Brough	Shed for 2.0 p.m.	
Stands		—	3	12 8	Beverley	11.20 a.m. Hornsea	11.35 Scarborough	
Stands		—	5	12 10	Withernsea	11.33 a.m. Scarborough	Station Pilot	
Withernsea		12 11	2	—	Stands	1.0 p.m. Beverley	Shed	
R.S.Q. ThO.		*12*12*	*5*	—	*South Sidings*	*B.C.L*	*Shed*	**Commences 22nd June*
Shed		—	1	12 12	North Cave	...	R.L.S.	
Shed		—	9	12 15	Brough	11.20 a.m. Goole	R.L.S.	
Withernsea Q. Ety.	S	12*15	Sdgs.	—	...	C Set	Shed	*Runs 1st to 31st Aug.
Shed		—	1	12 24	Beverley	11.6 a.m. Brough	R.L.S.	
Hornsea	S	12*23	1	—	Stands	12.40 p.m. Withernsea	Shed	*Not after 10th Sept.
Liverpool		12 27	9	—	Drawn	2.45 p.m. Liverpool	Shed for 2.45 p.m. Liverpool	
No. 4		—	10	12 30	Selby	11.45 a.m. Pontefract	Shed after arrival 11.45 a.m. from [Pontefract	
North Sidings		—	—	12 30	Billingsgate H. & B.	Engine and Van	Pilot	
Leeds		12 37	7	—	Stands	1.10 p.m. South Howden	Shed for 2.48 p.m. Leeds	
Stands	S	—	1	12 40*	Withernsea	*12.23 p.m. Hornsea	Station Pilot	*Not after 10th Sept.
Withernsea	S	12 40*	2	—	Stands	12.50 p.m. Hornsea	Shed	*Not after 10th Sept.
North Sidings		—	1	12*45	Beverley	8.31 a.m. Bridlington	Shed	*Not after 9th June
North Sidings		—	*5*	*12*45*	*Bridlington*	*8.31 a.m. Bridlington*	*Shed*	*Commences 12th June*
Shed		—	10	12 45	Brough	...	Diesel	
Liverpool, L.M.S.		12 49	5	—	South Sidings	6.40 p.m. Liverpool	Dairycoates	
Stands	S	—	2	12*50	Hornsea	12.40 p.m. Withernsea	Shed	*Not after 10th Sept.
Stands		—	8	1 0	Leeds	10.54 a.m. Leeds	Shed	
Stands		—	2	1 0	Beverley	12.11 p.m. Withernsea	Pilot	
Beverley		1 1	1	—	Shed	...	R.L.S.	
Stands		—	4	1 5	Brough	12.5 p.m. Sheffield	Shed	
North Sidings		—	*1*	*1 8*	*Withernsea, Th.O.*	*9.8 a.m. Brough*	*Dairycoates*	
Stands		—	7	1*10	South Howden	12.37 p.m. Leeds	Shed	*Hull dep. 1.11 p.m. [Th.O.
Fish Ex Billingsgate		1 10	—	—	F. Line	...	1.42 pm Withernsea	
Scarborough		1 7	2	—	Stands	1.42 p.m. Withernsea	Pilot to 2.30 p.m.	
North Sidings		—	3	1 15	Scarborough	8.38 a.m. Hornsea	Shed	
North Sidings		—	*1*	*1 20*	*Hornsea, Th.O.*	*9.5 a.m. Hornsea*	*Pilot*	
Brough		1 25	3	—	Shed	...	R.L.S.	
North Cave		1 26	1	—	Stands	1.45 p.m. Beverley	R.L.S.	
Beverley		1 30	4	—	Stands	1.45 p.m. Brough	Shed	
Leeds		1 36	7	—	No. 8	2.5 p.m. Leeds	Shed	
Brough		1 41	5	—	Stands	1.55 p.m. Willerby	Diesel	
Stands		—	2	1 42	Withernsea	1.7 p.m. Scarborough	Pilot from 12.30 p.m.	
Withernsea	S	1 43	1	—	North Sidings	5.35 p.m. Beverley	Shed & No. 35 Pilot	
Stands		—	1	1 45	Beverley	1.26 p.m. North Cave	R.L.S.	
Stands...		—	4	1 45	Brough	1.30 p.m. Beverley		
Hornsea		1 48	3	—	Stands	2.30 p.m. Bridlington	Pilot until 7.30 p.m.	
Shed		—	2	1*50	Hornsea	...	R.L.S.	*Steam Train from 29th May. 8.43 a.m. ex Goole
Stands		—	5	1 55	Willerby	1.41 p.m. Brough	Diesel	
Fish Ex Billingsgate FX		2 0	—	—	F. Line	...	...	Engine disposes of fish
York		2 0	2	—	North Sidings	5.20 p.m. Hornsea	Shed for 4.0pm Leeds	
South Sidings		—	6	2 0	Sheffield, Vic.	8.4 a.m. Doncaster 8.48 a.m. South Howden	Shed after arrival 12.5 p.m. ex Sheffield	
No. 7		—	8	2 5	Liverpool, L.M.S.	11.44 p.m. Leeds* 1.36 p.m. Leeds	Pilot	*Church Fenton BCL
Withernsea		2 9	7	—	Stands	2.48 p.m. Leeds	Shed	
Beverley		2 15	1	—	North Sidings	5.10 p.m. Leeds	Shed	
Brough		2 17	8	—	South Sidings	5.5 p.m. Doncaster	Pilot to 2.30 pm, then 5.40 pm With'nsea	
Hornsea	S	2 23	2	—	Stands	2.40 p.m. Withernsea	Shed	
Doncaster and King's Cross		2 25	4	—	South Sidings	5.30 p.m. Brough 5.5 p.m. King's Cross	Shed for 4.0 p.m. York	
Willerby		2 27	2	—	Shed	4.15 p.m. Goole	Diesel	
Liverpool, L.M.S.		2 29	6	—	Stands	4.0 p.m Liverpool	Shunts 2.30 p.m. to 3.45 and 5.0 p.m., then 5.48 p.m. [Leeds	
Stands		—	3	2 30	Bridlington	1.48 p.m. Hornsea	Shed	
Bridlington		2 30	5	—	Stands	3.15 p.m. Scarborough	Shed	*To 9th June
Scarborough W.O.	S	2 33	5	—	Stands	3.15 p.m. Scarborough	Shed & No. 35 Pilot	
Beverley		2*40	3	—	South Sidings	5.15 p.m. Beverley	Shed	
Stands	S	—	2	2 40	Withernsea	2.23 p.m. Hornsea	Shed	
Withernsea	S	2 42	3	—	Stands	2.50 p.m. Hornsea	Shed	

Arrivals at and Departures of Trains from the PARAGON STATION, and how dealt with—*continued*
MONDAYS TO FRIDAYS INCLUSIVE

FROM	Arr.	Platform	Dep.	TO	Set Working	Engine Working	Remarks
	p.m.		p.m.				
South Sidings No. 12 Platform after attaching wagons on rear and front	—	9	2 45	Liverpool	12.27 p.m. Liverpool	Shed after arrival 12.27 p.m. from Sheffield	
Stands	—	7	2 48	Leeds	2.9 p.m. Withernsea	Shed	
Brough	2 51	4	—	South Sidings	5.15 p.m. North Howden	Shed	
Stands S	—	3	2 50	Hornsea	2.42 p.m. Withernsea	Shed	
Hornsea, Th.O.	*2 59*	*2*	—	*North Sidings*	*5.35 p.m. Beverley*	*Shed*	
Beverley	3 1	3	—	Shed	3.45 p.m. Brough	R.L.S.	
South Howden	3 7	2	—	North Sidings	5.40 p.m. Withernsea	Shed	
Selby	3 12	8	—	Stands	3.25 p.m. York	Shed	
Withernsea, Th.O.	*3 12*	*4*	—	*To North Sidings*	*4.40 p.m. Brough*	*Shed*	
Stands	—	5	3 15	Scarborough	2.30 p.m. Bridlington	Shed	
Withernsea, Q.Ety. Th.O. S	3*16	Sdgs.	—	North Sidings	...	Shed	*Not after 29th July
Bridlington	*3*22*	*5*	—	*South Sidings*	*5.15 p.m. Beverley*	Shed for 4.30 p.m. Bridlington	**Commences 12th June*
Stands	—	8	3 25	York	3.12 p.m. Selby	Shed	
Hornsea	3*29	4	—	Shed	4.50 p.m. Hornsea	... [Sheffield	*Steam train from 29th May. 3.38 p.m. Withernsea
Newcastle	3 32	3	—	Stands	5.0 p.m. Newcastle	Shed for 4.32 p.m.	
Sheffield (Victoria)	3 36	8	—	Stands	4.30 p.m. Bridlington	Shed 5.0 p.m. York	
North Sidings	—	2	3 38	Withernsea	*8.43 a.m. Goole	...	*3.29 p.m. Hornsea from 29th May
Withernsea	3 46	5	—	Stands	4.20 p.m. Hornsea	Shed	
Shed	—	7	3 45	Brough	3.1 p.m. Beverley	R.L.S.	
North Sidings S	—	—	3†50	Scarborough Q	Spare Set	...	Runs when the 8.48 a.m. Relief is not run.
Sheffield (Victoria)	3 51	7	—	Stands	{4.32 p.m. Sheffield / 6.30 p.m. Manchester	Shed 5.5 p.m. Donc'r	Not after 9th Sept.
North Sidings	—	1	4 0	York	11.49 a.m. South Howden	Shed	
Stands	—	6	4 0	Liverpool, L.M.S.	2.26 p.m. Liverpool	Shed	
		14	4†5	Brough MWFO	Spare Set		
Shed	—	4	4 15	Goole	...	Diesel	
Stands	—	5	4 20	Hornsea	3.46 p.m. Withernsea	Shed	
Hornsea S	4 23	3	—	Stands	4.45 p.m. Beverley	Pilot	
Dairycoates	—	—	4†25	Brough	Spare Stock	Dairycoates	
Scarborough	4 25	1	—	Stands	4.40 p.m. Withernsea	Shed	
Shed	—	3	4 25	South Howden	...	R.L.S.	Top End
Stands	—	8	4 30	Bridlington	3.36 p.m. Sheffield	Shed	
Stands	—	7	4 32	Sheffield (Victoria)	3.51 p.m. Sheffield	Shed after arrival 3.26 p.m. from York	
Brough	4 36	10	—	Stands	5.17 p.m. North Cave	R.L.S.	
Withernsea S	4 37	8	—	Stands	5.15 p.m. Beverley	5.20 p.m. Hornsea	
Stands	—	1	4 40	Withernsea	4.25 p.m. Scarborough	Shed	
North Sidings	—	9	4 40	Brough	{9.8 a.m. Brough / 3.12 p.m. Withernsea Th.O.	Shed	
Walton Street	—	2	4 45	Beverley	C Set	Shed	Top End
Liverpool and Swansea	4 45	7	—	South Sidings	{6.30 p.m. Manchester / 10.35 a.m. Swansea	Shed for 6.30 p.m. Sheffield	
Shed	—	3	4*50	Hornsea	...	R.L.S.	*Steam train from 29th May. 8.52 a.m. Beverley
Stands	—	3	5 0	Newcastle	3.32 p.m. Newcastle	Shed after arrival 3.36 p.m. from Sheffield	
South Sidings	—	6	5 5	Doncaster and King's Cross	{2.17 p.m. Brough / 2.25 p.m. King's Cross	Shed after arr. 3.51 p.m. from Sheffield	
Leeds	5 8	7	—	Stands	5.48 p.m. Leeds	5.45 p.m. Beverley	
North Sidings	—	4	5 8	Scarborough	9.38 a.m. Scarborough	Shed	
North Sidings	—	5	5 10	Leeds	2.15 p.m. Beverley	Shed	
South Sidings	—	9	5 15	North Howden	2.51 p.m. Brough	Pilot	
South Sidings	—	8	5 15	Beverley	2*40 p.m. Beverley	Pilot for 1.30 p.m.	*3.22 p.m. Bridlington from 12th June
Liverpool, L.M.S.	5 15	5	—	Walton Street	9.15 a.m., Liverpool, L.M.S.	Shed for 6.40 p.m. [Wakefield	
Stands	—	10	5 17	North Cave	4.36 pm Brough	R.L.S.	
North Sidings	—	3	5 20	Hornsea	2.0 p.m. York	Shed	Top End
Sheffield and King's Cross	5 23	6	—	South Sidings	{9.18 p.m. Doncaster... [day / 11.45 a.m. King's Cross, next / 9.18 p.m. King's Cross	Pilot 5.30 p.m. to 7.0 p.m	
Walton Street	—	1	5 25	Withernsea	8.56 a.m. Withernsea	Train engine works own set Walton St. to No. 1 Platform, also pilot 1.45 to 3.40 p.m.	
South Sidings	—	8	5 30	Brough	2.25 p.m. Doncaster	Shed and platform own train	
Walton Street	—	2	5 30	Bridlington	8.59 a.m. Bridlington	Shed. Pilot 3.30 p.m	
Brough	5 31	14	—	Drawn	Made up Set	7.15 p.m. Brough	
Beverley	5 33	1	—	Stands	5.45 p.m. Beverley	5.50 p.m. Hornsea	
North Sidings	—	3	5 35	Beverley	{9.5 a.m. Hornsea Th.X / 2.59 p.m. Hornsea Th.O.	Shed	
Brough M.W.F.O.	5 36	4	—	Stands	6.45 p.m. Brough	5.55 p.m. S. Howden	
North Sidings	—	9	5 40	Withernsea	3.7 p.m. South Howden	Pilot	
South Sidings	—	*10*	*5*40*	*Riverside Quay W.O.*	*B.C.L.*	*Shed*	**Commences 17th June*
York	5 40	8	—	Stands	5.55 p.m. Pontefract	Shed for 7.30 p.m. York	
Brough M.W.F.O.	5 44	9	—	South Sidings	Spare Set		
Brough T.Th.O.	5 44	4	—	Stands	6.45 p.m. Beverley	5.55 p.m. S. Howden	
Withernsea	5 44	2	—	Stands	5.50 p.m. Hornsea	Shed	
Stands	—	1	5 45	Beverley	5.33 p.m. Beverley	5.8 p.m. Leeds	
Stands	—	7	5 48	Leeds	5.8 p.m. Leeds	Pilot 5.0 p.m. to 5.30 p.m.	
Stands	—	2	5 50	Hornsea	5.44 p.m. Withernsea	5.33 p.m. Beverley	
Beverley	5 50	1	—	Stands	6.5 p.m. Scarborough	6.25 p.m. With'sea	
Stands	—	8	5 55	Pontefract	5.40 p.m. York	Shed	
North Sidings	—	5	5 55	South Howden	B.C.L. and T.		
Doncaster	5 58	8	—	Stands	6.15 p.m. Brough	6.15 p.m. Brough	
Hornsea	6 3	2	—	Stands	6.18 p.m. Hornsea	6.18 p.m. Hornsea	
Stands	—	1	6 5	Scarborough	5.50 p.m. Beverley	Shed	
Scarborough	6 6	6	—	Stands	6.25 p.m. Withernsea	Shed	
Walton Street	—	*14*	*6 10*	*Bridlington, Excn. Th.O.*	*Spare Stock*	*Dairycoates*	*Commences 1st June*
Billingsgate Q	6 10	Yard	—	Via Walton Street	Fish Pilot		
R.S. Quay † W.O.	*6*11*	*F Line*	—	*Sidings*	*B.C.L.*	*Shed*	**Commences 17th June*
Shed	—	1	6 15	Beverley	...	R.L.S.	Trailer attached
Stands	—	8	6 15	Brough	5.58 p.m. Doncaster	5.58 p.m. Doncaster	
Stands	—	2	6 18	Hornsea	6.3 p.m. Hornsea	6.3 p.m. Hornsea	
Leeds	6 21	8	—	Stands	8.40 p.m. Leeds	Shed Pilot 7.30 p.m. to 8.30 p.m.	
Hornsea	6*21	1	—	Shed	...	R.L.S.	*Steam Train from 29th May. 5.44 a.m. Withernsea
Stands	—	6	6 25	Withernsea	6.6 p.m. Scarborough	5.50 p.m. Beverley	
Beverley	6 30	5	—	Walton Street	7.15 a.m. York	Shed	
South Sidings	—	9	6 30	Sheffield (Victoria) and Manchester	{4.45 p.m. Liverpool / 3.51 p.m. Manchester	Shed	
Brough	6 33	3	—	Stands	6.45 p.m. Beverley	6.45 p.m. Beverley	
South Howden	6 33	1	—	Stands	6.55 p.m. South Howden	R.L.S.	
York	6 37	6	—	Stands	7.30 p.m. York	Shed	
North Sidings	—	10	6 40	Wakefield, L.M.S.	12.49 p.m. Liverpool, L.M.S.	Shed	
Withernsea	6 43	2	—	Stands	7.10 p.m. Scarborough	Pilot	
Goole	6 44	9	—	Shed	7†0 p.m. Brough T.Th.O.	Diesel	
Stands	—	3	6 45	Beverley	6.33 p.m. Brough	6.33 p.m. Brough	
Stands	—	4	6 45	Brough	*5.36 p.m. Brough	Pilot and 9.57 p.m. Beverley	*5.44 p.m. Brough T.Th.O

Arrivals at and Departures of Trains from the PARAGON STATION, and how dealt with—*continued*
MONDAYS TO FRIDAYS INCLUSIVE

FROM	Arr	Platform	Dep	TO	Set Working	Engine Working	Remarks
	p.m.		p.m.				
Beverley	6 50	4	—	Stands	7.13 p.m. Hornsea	Pilot	
Stands	—	1	6 55	South Howden	6.33 p.m. South Howden	R.L.S.	
Stands	—	14	7†5	Brough T.Th.O.	Spare Set		
Stands	—	2	7 10	Scarborough	6.43 p.m. Withernsea	Shed	
Beverley	7 3	1	—	Shed	...	R.L.S.	
North Howden	7 5	7	—	Stands	7.15 p.m. Brough	7.25 p.m. With'nsea	
North Cave	7 9	5	—	Shed	8.45 p.m. Beverley	R.L.S.	
Stands	—	4	7 13	Hornsea	6.50 p.m. Beverley	Shed	
Bridlington*	7 15	2	—	Stands	7.25 p.m. Withernsea	Shed	*From Scarborough from 29th May
Stands	—	7	7‡15	Brough	7.5 p.m. North Howden	{5.31 p.m. Brough / Shed. Dairycoates	M.W.F.O / ‡To Leeds T.Th.O.
Stands	—	2	7 25	Withernsea	7.15 p.m. Bridlington		
Hornsea	7 25	1	—	North Sidings	6.44 a.m. Goole	Pilot	
Beverley	7 30	2	—	South Sidings	7.30 a.m. Sheffield	Shed	
Stands	—	6	7 30	York	6.37 p.m. York	Shed after arr. 5.40 p.m. from York	
Liverpool	7 37	7	—	Walton Street	8.55 a.m. Liverpool	Shed	
Brough	7 40	5	—	North Sidings	6.23 a.m. South Howden	Shed	
Withernsea	7 38	4	—	Stands	8.5 p.m. Selby	Shed	
Scarborough S	7 42	3	—	North Sidings	6.50 a.m. Hornsea	Shed	
Liverpool, L.M.S.	7 43	6	—	Walton Street	9.0 a.m. Liverpool, L.M.S.	Pilot to midnight	
York	7 57	3	—	North Sidings	7.10 a.m. Arram	Shed	
Brough T.Th.O.	7 58	5	—	Drawn	7.0 a.m. Brough	Shed	
South Howden	8 0	1	—	North Sidings	B.C.L. and T.	Shed	
Brough M.W.F.O.	8 2	5	—	Drawn	7.0 a.m. Brough	Shed	
Stands	—	4	8 5	Selby	7.38 p.m. Withernsea	Shed & No. 35 Pilot	
Scarborough	8 11	2	—	Stands	9.15 p.m. Bridlington	Shed	
Withernsea Th.O. S	8*11	7	—	North Sidings	C Set	Shed. Dairycoates	*Runs 4th to 25th Aug.
King's Cross	8 13	4	—	No. 10	11.30 a.m. King's Cross	Shed	Pullman
Brough T.Th.O.	8 17	—	—	South Sidings	Spare Set	Shed	
Shed	—	1	8 20	Beverley	...	R.L.S.	
Brough M.W.F.O.	8†22	F line	—	South Sidings	6.50 a.m. Hornsea	Shed. Dairycoates	
Hornsea	8 26	5	—	Stands	9.5 p.m. Hornsea	Shed	
Withernsea S	8*34	3	—	Stands	9.12 p.m. Withernsea	Shed	**Not after 27th Aug.*
Pontefract	8 40	4	—	No. 10	9.25 a.m. Pontefract	Shed for 9.40 p.m. Selby	
Stands	—	8	8 40	Leeds and Pontefract	{4.15 a.m. Pontefract / 6.21 p.m. Leeds	Shed. Pilot 7.30 to 8.30 p.m.	
Withernsea Q. Rlf. S	8*41	4	—	North Sidings	C. Set	Shed [from Leeds	*Q 1st to 31st Aug.
Shed	—	1	8 45	Beverley	7.9 p.m. North Cave	R.L.S.	
Scarborough Q. Rlf. S	8*48	4	—	Drawn	C Set	...	*Runs 1st to 31st Aug.
Hornsea Rlf. Q S	8*50	5	—	Stands	9*5 Hornsea	Shed	*Not after 27th Aug.
Beverley S	8†52	2	—	Shed	...	R.L.S.	
South Howden	8 55	8	—	Stands	9.45 p.m. Brough	R.L.S.	
Manchester and Doncaster	8 56	6	—	Stands	{10.53 p.m. Sheffield / 8.55 a.m. Manchester	Pilot to 10.50 p.m.	
Bridlington S	9 1	4	—	Drawn	...	Shed	
Beverley	9 1	1	—	Shed	...	R.L.S.	
Stands	—	5	9 5	Hornsea	8.26 p.m. Hornsea	No. 34 Pilot	
Withernsea	9 6	3	—	Stands	9.12 p.m. Withernsea	Pilot to 5.0 a.m.	
Scarborough	*9*8*	*1*	—	*North Sidings*	*10.40 a.m. Scarborough*	*9.57 p.m. Beverley*	*Commences 29th May*
Stands	—	3	9 12	Withernsea	9.6 p.m. Withernsea	Pilot	
Stands	—	2	9 15	Bridlington	8.11 p.m. Scarborough	Shed	
South Sidings	—	9	9 18	Doncaster	{5.23 p.m. Doncaster / 5.23 p.m. King's Cross	Shed	
Beverley W.O. Ety R.L.S. S	9 22	7	—	Stands	9.45 p.m. Brough	R.L.S.	
Hornsea	9 25	5	—	Stands	10.15 p.m. Brough	Shed	
Beverley	9 31	2	—	Stands	9.55 p.m. North Cave	R.L.S.	
Bridlington W.O. S	9 31	4	—	Shed	10.50 p.m. Bridlington	Shed	
Withernsea	9 43	3	—	Stands	9.57 p.m. Beverley	Shed	
Stands	—	8	9 45	Brough	8.55 p.m. South Howden	R.L.S.	
King's Cross and Doncaster	9 48	9	—	Middle Sidings	9.30 a.m. King's Cross	Dairycoates	
Scarborough Q. S	9*48	4	—	South Sidings	Made up Set	Shed	*Runs 2nd August to 13th September
Bridlington W.O.	*9 51*	1	—	*Shed*	*11.23 Bridlington W.O.*	*R.L.S.*	
Stands	—	2	9 55	North Cave	9.31 p.m. Beverley	R.L.S.	
Stands	—	3	9 57	Beverley	9.43 p.m. Withernsea	Shed	
Scarborough	10 0	2	—	Stands T.Th.O. / North Sidings M.W.F.O.	{6†30 a.m. Withernsea T.Th.X. / 11.20 p.m. Withernsea T.Th.O.	Shed	
Church Fenton	10 12	3	—	Stands	10.30 p.m. Beverley	Shed	
Stands	—	5	10 15	Brough	9.25 p.m. Hornsea	R.L.S.	
Stands	—	3	10 30	Beverley	10.12 p.m. Church Fenton	Shed	
Sheffield	10 31	8	—	Walton Street	5.58 a.m. Sheffield	11.23 p.m. Beverley	W.S.X.
York	10 35	2	—	Middle Sidings	11.45 a.m. King's Cross	Pilot T.Th.O. 10.50 p.m. to 12.0 mid.	
Scarborough S	10*44	3	—	Stands	11.26 p.m. Hornsea T.Th.O.	Shed	*Not after 10th Sept.
Beverley	10 52	7	—	North Sidings	5.50 a.m. Scarborough		
Stands	—	6	10 53	Sheffield (Vict.)	8.56 p.m. Sheffield	Dairycoates	
Hornsea	11 6	3	—	Stands	11.23 p.m. Beverley W.X	11.23 p.m. Beverley	W.X.
North Cave	11 7	6	—	Shed	...	R.L.S.	
Beverley	11 10	5	—	Stands	{11.26 p.m. Hornsea T.Th.O. / 5.40 a.m. Leeds T.Th.X.	Shed	
King's Cross	11 15	9	—	Stands	9.30 a.m. King's Cross	Shed	
Withernsea	11 15	6	—	North Sidings	7.40 a.m. Withernsea	Shed	
Stands	—	*2*	*11 20*	*Withernsea T.Th.O.*	*10.0 p.m. Scarborough*	*Pilot*	
Scarborough S	11 22	6	—	North Sidings	6.50 a.m. Hornsea	Shed. Dairycoates	W.S.X.
Stands	—	3	11 23	Beverley W.X.	11.6 p.m. Hornsea	10.31 p.m. Sheffield	
Shed	—	*1*	*11 23*	*Bridlington W.O.*	*9.51 p.m. Bridlington*	R.L.S.	
Brough	11 24	7	—	North Sidings	7.45 a.m. Beverley		
Stands	—	*5*	*11 26*	*Hornsea T.Th.O.*	11.10 p.m. Beverley	10.52 p.m. Beverley	
Bridlington Exc. Th.O.	11*41	3	—	Walton Street	Spare Stock	Shed	*Commences 1st Juue
Leeds	11 56	2	—	South Sidings	6.50 a.m. Hornsea	Shed	Two Sets. T.Th.O.
Beverley W.X.	12†4	3	—	...	...	Pilot to 3.0 a.m.	

Saturday train workings were similar to the above weekday workings whilst Sunday activity was curtailed to about a third of that listed above.

A smoke screen goes up from V3 67684 as it passes St.Andrews Dock box with the 4.20 p.m. Paragon – Brough stopper on 25th February 1963. Photograph Peter Rose.

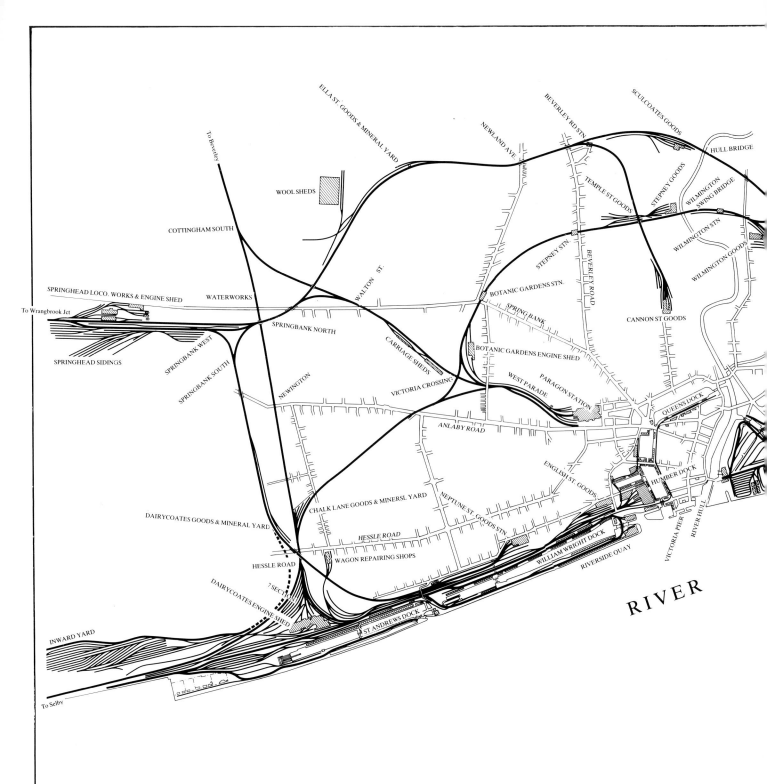

To handle the ever increasing coal traffic for the Humber docks it was necessary to make further alterations in the Priory Siding area. As part of this work the passenger lines were elevated onto a new embankment, commencing just behind Hessle Road signalbox, and extending for about 1¼ miles towards Hessle East Junction. Slightly less than halfway along its length the mineral lines giving access between the coal sidings and the docks were crossed by means of a 179 foot span girder bridge. The work, when finished, formed part of an extensive scheme of reception loops, sorting and empty mineral sidings. In all, the total length of the completed works was 75 miles, with a capacity of 10,784 wagons. The new bridge and embankment is predominant in this view looking almost due east, of June 7th 1984. At ground level and leading to the left is the already severed North branch; until a few months previously this formed a connection to Hessle Road. The signal had the dubious honour of being the last example of a working semaphore in the city and, like its controlling signal box Dairycoates West, just visible through the bridge span, was taken out of use from Sunday 10th June 1984. Photograph Mick Nicholson.

HULL

Railways and Docks 1947

Scale 2.2 inches equals 1 mile approx.

To Hornsea

DANSON LANE

BURLEIGH ST. GOODS

HOLDERNESS ROAD

HOLDERNESS DRAIN NORTH

MARFLEET STATION

SOUTHCOATES STN.

SOUTHCOATES LANE

SEWARD ST. GOODS

HEDON ROAD

To Withernsea

TORIA DOCK

ALEXANDRA DOCK

KING GEORGE DOCK

TIMBER STORGE AREA

HUMBER

SALT END

OIL TENANCIES

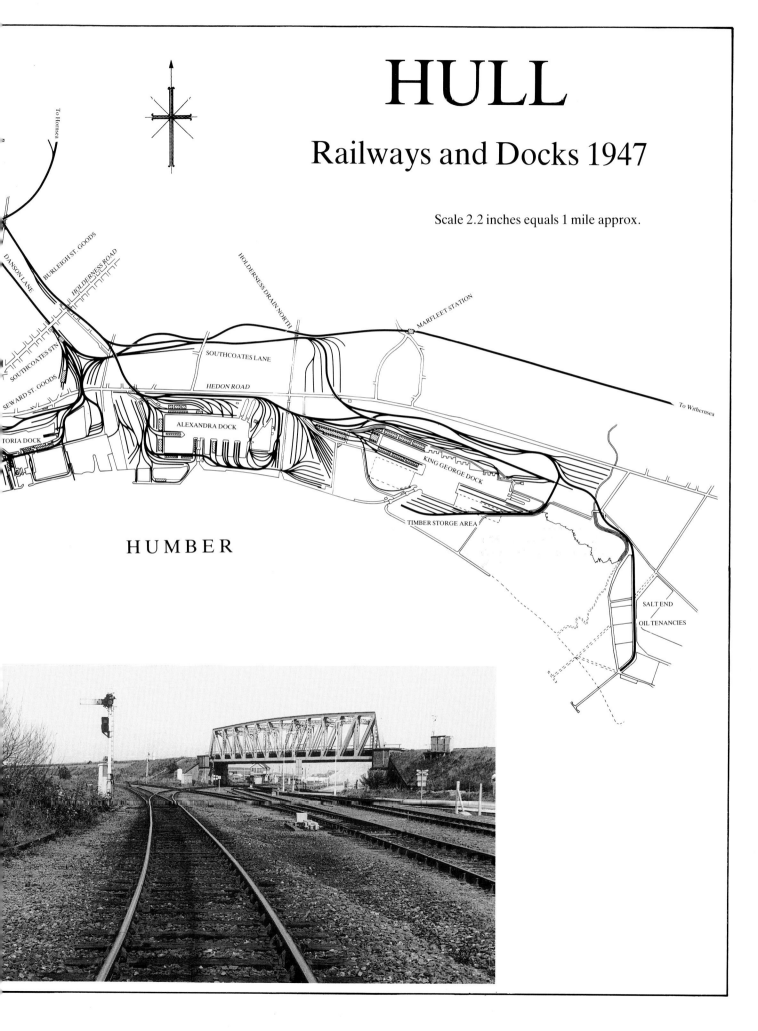

In the next six years Hull's railways took a two-fold hammering at a time when only the very minimum of maintenance could be provided, with the nightly blackout only adding to the difficulties of 'carrying on'. There were 82 air raids on Hull during World War Two and of these 21 brought significant damage to railway installations; of the city's 91,000 houses, 86,000 had notifiable damage and railway employees would be concerned with a good proportion of them. Yet, 'work–related stress' was then either unknown or just had to be ignored and endured for six long, weary years. Paragon station itself was only slightly damaged, but grievously, the small local railway museum which had been established in one of its upstairs rooms was completely burned out by incendiaries.

Nationalisation, effective from January 1st 1948, changed the Hull railway scene relatively little, although we then ceased to see engines from what we had regarded as 'foreign' companies. Until the 1914 war there was a daily arrival and departure of a London & North Western Railway engine (usually a Precursor class 4–4–0 on the Liverpool Lime Street service) but after 1918, LNWR engines only came to Hull on specials. One which did had an unhappy arrival. On Saturday February 5th 1927, No 136 MINERVA of that railway's 'Prince of Wales' class, bringing in a ten coach Rugby League excursion from Halifax, was in side-long collision with the five coach 12.59 p.m. passenger train from Hornsea, due to the conductor–driver of the 4–6–0 over–running his signal, outside Paragon station. Fortunately, casualties were limited to slight injuries, suffered by two passengers

in the Hornsea train and one in the Halifax train. The train with the right of way had pushed the 107 ton LNWR engine and tender off the rails. Interestingly they were still in LNWR black painting even after more than four years of LMS ownership.

The Lancashire & Yorkshire Railway outstationed a goods engine at Dairycoates shed, and one of their passenger engines took out the 9.12 a.m. express from Paragon Station to Wakefield, Manchester (Victoria) and Liverpool (Exchange). Both the L&Y, and the LNWR engines had lined black painting – in distinct contrast to the Saxony green of the North Eastern passenger engines to which we were accustomed.

Until after the Grouping, the darker green of Great Central passenger engines could be seen daily in Paragon Station. A 4–4–0, outstationed in Hull, worked the 7.50 a.m. through train to Sheffield (Victoria) and there were also through expresses which, in 1922, arrived in Hull at 5.31 p.m. and went back at 6.20 p.m. So we did not lack variety in those days.

The same painting after 1923 was applied to engines which had been owned by the North Eastern, Hull & Barnsley, Great Northern, Great Central, and Great Eastern Railways, examples of which all worked into Paragon Station. Those which had belonged to the Lancashire & Yorkshire went into the London Midland & Scottish group, and although their major passenger engines were painted red, those which continued to work the Wakefield, Manchester and Liverpool trains to and from Hull only qualified for black paint. Sadly, that sombre garb became increasingly applied to LNER passenger engines, especially after painting economies were

introduced from April 1928.

Even so, we still had wide variety of engines to maintain our interest – from 1923 to 1939 many LNER classes worked into Hull, which had originally been designed for services in very different parts of the country. Great Northern Atlantics (both large and small boilered), 4–4–0s and 4–4–2 tanks were seen in Paragon daily, whilst at Dairycoates GN 'Long Tom' 0–8–0 goods engines of class Q2, and the Q3 singleton could be seen on Sundays, resting before working back to Nottingham and West Riding sheds. Enthusiasm equal to that of bird watchers was generated when ex–Great Eastern engines appeared, and as a result local photographers got 1561E (in 1924) a B12/1, 8037 (D13) in 1925, 8817 (D16/3) in 1934, and (a distinct *rara avis*) 8292 (J20) in 1937. Great Central classes working goods trains from Colwick and Ardsley included B6, B7, and B9 classes, and instead of the usual 4–4–0 we occasionally got a B2 (Sir Sam Fay) and B8 (Glenalmond) 4–6–0 class; the B2 still in fully lined green.

Having considered the interesting visitors, we must now deal with the home team of engines with which we were daily acquainted. Just as rat catchers have now to be called rodent operators, what we knew as engine sheds also went up market to become Motive Power Depots. Hull was generously provided with four of them, and when I began to visit them in 1933 there were some 300 engines to keep tabs on. First however, we must dispose of two other Hull sheds, of which nobody now living can possibly have any memory. Perhaps there might even have been another one, or at least some shelter for the Hull

From 1869 the Lancashire & Yorkshire Railway had running powers over the NER to work into Hull. Naturally this agreement was continued by the LMS, and in one form or another remained in use until nationalisation. Even beyond 1948, as we have seen elsewhere, inter–regional workings did from time to time bring interesting and varied motive power within the city. In this nicely framed view a stranger is caught in the shape of an L&Y Dreadnaught 4–6–0. Actually 10464 was always LMS property as she didn't roll out of Horwich works until October 1924. Apart from the LMS Central Division reporting number C740 on the smokebox we have no other clue to what this working was, almost 60 years ago. The location, Dairycoates, indicates arrival at the head of a goods job, having come from the West Riding via Staddlethorpe Junction. 10464 was destined not to last long after this late 1930s picture, and met its doom during June 1939. Photograph Jim Proud.

and Selby engines in the years 1840–48, when they worked out of Manor House station – if so, I have found no documentary evidence.

When Paragon station opened in 1848, a three road 'Engine House' was also built, adjoining the station wall on the north side. In 1865 (soon enlarged, in 1867) a new shed, further away to the north was built. In 1876 an additional shed adjoining the existing one was opened to house a further twenty engines. The north wall of the three bay shed was then in close proximity to the south transept of the church of St. Stephen's, and we are fortunate in having a photograph showing church, and shed. The turn of the century extensions to Paragon station took in the 'Engine House' and also required the site of Paragon shed, so in replacement, Botanic Gardens shed was built about half a mile away by the side of the Victoria Dock branch. It was erected on ground which had been occupied by a lunatic asylum; closed in 1892, it's buildings were demolished in 1898. When Botanic Gardens shed was opened, early in 1901, demolition of the Paragon shed began in the May. Botanic Gardens, like its predecessor, housed mainly passenger engines. From its 1854 opening, the Hull and Holderness Railway was operated by hired engines but in 1858 the company bought one of their own, and decided to erect a shed for it. After the July 1862 absorption by the North Eastern, they referred to that small shed as Hull (Drypool), but it became redundant following the 1864 transfer of Withernsea trains from Victoria Dock station to Paragon station. So in 1866 it was taken down and moved to Lockington (on the Bridlington line north of Beverley), for use as a goods shed.

Dairycoates shed, which ultimately became the largest on the North Eastern, was two miles from Paragon but that was no handicap, for it dealt almost entirely with goods, fish, and mineral trains, yard shunting, and local trip working, both in the city and also to and from all the docks.

No 1 roundhouse was opened in 1863 and Nos 2 and 3 (which had 50 foot turntables) were added in 1876; even so in a 1913 Sunday afternoon photograph, at least 64 engines can be identified as having to be stabled in the open, and not under cover. In that year, extensions were already being constructed, and they added three more roundhouses, each with a 60 foot turntable – also two straight sheds, one housing a double track elevated wheel drop, and the other the 25 ton breakdown crane. Concurrently, the NER designed, and Spencers of Melksham built, a mechanically operated coaling plant. Although not the first in the country, it was an improved design, and in early LNER years, it was coaling an average of 166 engines a day. Construction was

Visiting Q2 No.3410 spends a quiet Sunday inside Dairycoates roundhouse before working back to the coalfields with mineral empties.

A rare bird indeed. J20 No.8292 came a long way from its usual habitat in former Great Eastern territory in 1937.

sufficiently robust for it to see (almost – a JCB substituted for the 'Coal Cracker' at the last) the end of steam engines at Dairycoates, in June 1967, and shortly thereafter it was demolished.

Water quality was a prime factor in the performance and maintenance of boilers on steam engines, and the Hull area is notorious for hard water, most of it coming from boreholes in the chalk of the Yorkshire Wolds, with a consequent high lime content. This was counteracted from 1902 by the erection of a large softening plant, in Hessle station yard; doubling its size in 1908 enabled it to supply all the North Eastern Railway requirements throughout the Hull area, including the Dairycoates and Botanic Gardens sheds, and the Para-gon station water cranes.

After the Dairycoates shed (sorry – Motive Power Depot) closed, the roundhouses were rented off for industrial use, but the straight shed with wheel drop was rented by a group of enthusiasts who formed Humberside Locomotive Preservation Group. Their high quality work can best be judged by the reliability that they have conferred on LMS 'Black Five' No 5305, the King Arthur SIR LAMIEL and the 1899–built Great Northern 0–6–0 tank No 1247. Because of a recent plan to demolish the roundhouses, to cash in on their site value, the HLPG has had to vacate the wheeldrop shed and squeeze into the breakdown crane shed, where it will only be able to tackle coaches, so long as it can survive.

The former H&B erecting shop at Springhead. Capable of the heaviest repairs, the place was somewhat under utilised by the LNER.

Botanic Gardens shed dates from 1901, and until it closed to steam on June 14th 1959, it was the home of the passenger engines operating the services out of Paragon station. Those took them to Leeds, Doncaster, Sheffield, Scarborough, York, Hornsea, and Withernsea, none more than 60 miles, and in only three places were there major gradients to tackle. The Yorkshire Wolds had to be crossed on the lines to Scarborough, and to York, and on the Leeds line the ridge between Milford and Micklefield needed hard work, the trains to and from Leeds being the most heavily loaded.

For coaling the engines, until 1932 a standard pattern North Eastern coal stage served, which meant hand shovelling into small trucks, which were then wheeled and tipped as required. That chore was then superseded through the introduction of a mechanical plant, its single bunker filled by rail wagons hoisted, tipped and emptied of their contents. In connection with the mid–1950s change to diesel railcars, the shed buildings were demolished in 1956/57, although at first, the existing turntables and stalls were retained, and steam

engines continued to use the shed until June 1959, when those remaining were finally transferred to Dairycoates. The building has served for 30 years, but latterly has only been used for refuelling and minor maintenance, a 1988 British Railways rationalisation leading to the concentration of diesel powered vehicles on Neville Hill shed, at Leeds.

When Hull's own railway to thwart the North Eastern's monopoly began operation in July 1885, the main Hull and Barnsley engine shed was located at Springhead on the western outskirts, some three miles from the city centre. The shed was a straight one, open at both ends, and after it had been extended in 1890 and 1897, and lengthened by 200 feet in 1907, it had eight through lines. The 1890 additions included a water softening plant, and those of 1907 a high level, but manually operated coaling stage, also a new 55 foot turntable. Well equipped erecting, boiler, and repair shops were built north of the running shed, and whilst no new locomotives were ever built, the place was capable of dealing with the heaviest of repairs. There was even a small drawing office, from which the single

draughtsman was transferred to Darlington in 1922, when the North Eastern took over, and where, in the 1950s, he became Chief of the much larger and more important Drawing Office.

The working of passenger trains was always a secondary duty at Springhead and that ceased entirely with the diversion of such trains from Cannon Street to Paragon on July 14th 1924. The H & B's five 4–4–0s were then transferred to Botanic Gardens shed, from where they worked to withdrawal in 1933 and 1934.

By far the major reason for bringing the Hull and Barnsley into being was to export coal through the company's Alexandra Dock, and Springhead's fortunes and activity fluctuated according to the amount of that traffic. From 1½ million tons of coal moved in 1903, it grew to 4½ millions in 1913, then dropped to about 1¼ millions in the war years. By 1924 there had been recovery to 2¼ millions, but the six months coal strike of 1926 began a decline to an annual average of about a million tons. This was halted completely by the 1939 war. Springhead shed became increasingly neglected after the war, especially the maintenance of its roof. In the mid–1950s, half the shed was reroofed to make it suitable for housing diesel railcars, the sixteen remaining steam engines then being confined to the other four roads, which became increasingly open to the weather. The shed was at last officially closed to steam on December 15th 1958, although the engines had moved away on November 30th. The shed continued to be a signing on point for crews, and was used to maintain diesel locos and railcars, but even that ceased in July 1961, and today the whole Springhead complex is just open ground. Standing there, it is almost beyond comprehension that in 1922 the number employed there was 1,220, employment that has just disappeared.

It is of interest to consider what that employment meant to one man who spent all his 49 years working life there. When the Hull and Barnsley opened in 1885, engine drivers had to be recruited from all across the country. Understandably perhaps, the North Eastern did not encourage any of its staff to join the rival system and men had to be persuaded to move to Hull from whatever part of the country they happened to live. From the Great Northern at Peterborough came not only Matthew Stirling to be the Company's only Chief Mechanical Engineer, but also a driver named Gregory. As was customary with railway employees, his son J. George Gregory followed in his work on the Hull and Barnsley, in 1901, and by 1933, when I first met him, he had risen to be shedmaster at Springhead, a post that he kept to retirement in 1952. He gave me much documentary information, amongst which is his shed note book for the years 1922 to 1925. Personal entries show that the company provided him with an overcoat on December 1st 1921, and a macintosh on the 16th. Then on March 2nd 1923 he was issued with leggings and a replacement overcoat. His first job when he started at 6.00 a.m. in those early 1920s was to note which engines on shed were stopped for repairs, and the reason. The day's work facing him on Monday February 1st 1926 is quite a typical example, with 43 engines needing his organisation to get them running in traffic again as quickly as possible. His list for that day runs as follows:– 2407 Tubes; 2503/40/42, 2409 and 2243 Boiler Repairs; 2500 Boiler & Wheels; 2430/32 to be scrapped; 2520, 2472, 1032, 1002, Boiler Repairs; 2518 Intermediate Buffers; 1311 Hot Box; 2420 Regulator Valve; 2530 Washout Plugs; 2247 Main Steampipe; 2515 Conn. Rod; 2446 Intermediate Buffers; 2453 Glands; 2504/09/35/37, 2440 Loose Tyres; 1136 Springs; 2230, 2510, 1292, 2411/19 Hot Box; 2443 Crankpin; 2411/74 Tender Wheels; 2454/95 Loose Wheels; 2447 Cylinder Repairs; 2460 R.H.Valve Spindle; 2464 Crankpin; 2444 Snow Plough; 262 Motion

Repairs; 2413 Side Rods. Whilst he was supervising this wide variety of repairs, there would be frequent telephone calls from the traffic staff asking when they could have an engine for a particular goods, or mineral empties. That was the daily round – every day. We as enthusiasts usually only saw engines when they were in running condition and gave little thought to those whose job was to keep them that way.

The fourth Hull shed, Alexandra Dock, probably epitomised the life of the Hull and Barnsley Railway. To work the quays, jetties, and coal hoists, engines Nos 1 to 12 were 0–6–0 tanks, built 1885. Their shed was a two road structure which was probably all that the company could afford at the time. These engines had worked hard, for long hours, and were rapidly approaching their sell–by date when they became North Eastern Railway property in 1922. The North Eastern immediately withdrew Nos 1 to 12 and the six 0–4–0Ts, replacing them by engines of the same wheel arrangement from its own stock. No 1 was actually cut up outside Springhead in 1923, but five of the 0–6–0s were sold for £350 each to Tyneside collieries for further work, and the wheels, frames, and working parts of 0–4–0 No 48 were presented to Hull Technical College where, its curious valve gear mystified students until it disappeared in a metal salvage drive during the 1939–45 war. The shed building had been declared beyond repair in 1913 and, as our illustration shows, was even more ramshackle and decrepit in 1922, because nothing had been – or ever was – done to it. During 1927, the wood structure just had to be demolished, but no replacement was provided. From October 1953, its 350 h.p. diesel shunters

just stood in the open air, over the pits in the two roads which had originally been inside the shed. From late 1953 there was a gradual changeover to diesel shunters, but steam lingered on for seven more years, until the last steam engines left for Dairycoates in November 1960. The diesels followed on October 27th 1963, a result of a down–turn in trade exacerbated by the restrictive practices of the dockers. Alexandra Dock itself closed completely at the end of November 1983, ships having ceased to use it from September 1982. In February 1988, Bridge No.1 over Hedon Road, and in November 1988, Bridge No.4 over New Bridge Road, were dismantled, thus effectively cutting off rail access to the dock. However the abolition of the Dock Labour Scheme in 1989 removed a great handicap, and Alexandra Dock, after some rehabilitation and a considerable amount of dredging, was able to be ceremonially reopened on July 16th 1991, the 106th anniversary of its original opening. Sadly, that does not concern our account further, because rail access to it has not been restored.

On June 25th 1967 the last two steam engines in Hull were transferred away; these were B1 class 61306 which went to Low Moor, and WD class 90009, to Sunderland.

J71 No.225 alongside the delapidated wooden shed that served the Alexandra Dock locomotive fleet. Photograph R. Copeman.

ADDITIONAL STATION PROVIDED BY BR

The goods line which the Hull and Barnsley had built in 1885, from Spring Bank South junction to its Neptune Street goods depot was adjacent to the new football ground to which Hull City A.F.C. had moved in 1946. The 1924 spur from the H & B line to Walton Street junction enabled trains to be run directly from Paragon station to the goods line at the side of the football ground – so on January 6th 1951, Boothferry Park station was opened. Using 12,000 pre–cast concrete units, in nine weeks a single platform was built, 600 feet long and 10 feet wide with a ramp leading down directly to turnstiles. For maximum load capacity on the 8 or 9 minute journey, the trains used 8 coaches made up of two 'quad–art' sets borrowed from the G.N. London suburban area, hauled by either a B1 class 4–6–0, (61080 hauled the first one) or a 4MT 2–6–0 from Dairycoates shed. On February 3rd 1951, my engine on the 2.25 p.m. from Paragon station was 43053, with 43076 on the 5.05 p.m. return. On December 6th 1952 they were 43078 outward, but 61267 on the return. That was a Bradford B1 which Dairycoates had 'borrowed' – not an unusual occurrence, and they repeated it for me on January 17th 1953 with 61296, also belonging to Bradford shed.

On the opening day, eight trains at ten minute intervals were provided, and they carried 4,920 passengers, who further enjoyed Hull City beating Everton 2–0. When the match finished at 3.55 p.m. five trains were waiting, and with one making a double trip, they had cleared the returning passengers by 4.29 p.m. Only return tickets could be obtained, and the fare – which now seems incredible – was sixpence. Patronage remained high through the 1950s, but then gradually dwindled, as Hull City have never managed to become a fashionable club able to draw big crowds regularly. The Boothferry Park special train service ceased to be operated at the end of the 1985/6 football season, although the station has not yet (1993) been closed officially, and the platform is still available should it ever be required, but this seems unlikely.

STOCK EXHIBITIONS IN HULL

In December 1927 friends of the local hospital in Blyth persuaded railwaymen to organise a show of rolling stock on a Sunday for fund raising. The idea proved to be so successful that by 1939 some fifty similar events had taken place at LNER stations. Redcar had a small one on January 2nd 1928, and Newcastle a big one three weeks later. Hull were the next to organise one, in platforms 1 and 2 of Paragon station, on March 25th 1928, when 23,543 attended and raised over £500 for the NER Cottage Homes. There was an official opening by the Lord Mayor, with LNER Director, Major W.H. Carver presiding; music was provided by the NUR military band.

The main exhibit was A1 Pacific No 2569 GLADIATEUR, straight from repair and rep-aint at Darlington, a far larger engine than was to work into the station for at least another ten years. It brought with it a museum item, Tennant 2–4–0 No 1463 having been newly restored to its 1885 original North Eastern livery only three days before the exhibition, so it made its debut as a historical locomotive in Hull. 65 years later, you can still see it in Darlington North Road Museum, but GLADIATEUR was

In Aid of the **N.E.R. Cottage Homes and Benefit Fund, the Railway Servants' Orphanage, Derby and Local Charities.**

EXHIBITION

of the Latest

PACIFIC AND OTHER TYPES OF ENGINES DINING AND SLEEPING CARS, ETC.

EXPRESS PASSENGER ENGINE, L. & N.E.R " SHIRE CLASS "
(By kind permission of the North Mail and Newcastle Chronicle)

PARAGON STATION, HULL - Platform Nos. 1 & 2,
Sunday, 25th March, 1928

THE LORD MAYOR OF HULL (Alderman Herbert Dean, J.P.) accompanied by the SHERIFF (Samuel Webster, Esq.) will perform the Opening Ceremony

at 10 a.m.

MAJOR W. H. CARVER, M.P., J.P., Director of the London & North Eastern Railway Coy. will preside.

Admission by Ticket. *Adults* **6d.** *Children under* 16, **3d.**

Selections of Music will be rendered by the Hull N.U.R. Band at intervals.

Tickets can be obtained at the Booking Office, Paragon Station (No. 4 Window), at all Stations in the District, and on the day of the Exhibition at the Temporary Office on the Platform.

Cheap Tickets will be issued to Hull from certain stations.
For particulars see L. & N.E.R. announcements.

The Exhibition will close at 8 p.m.   For further information apply at any Booking Office.

PARAGON STATION, HULL.
21st February, 1928.

Refreshments can be obtained at the Station Refreshment Room.

to disappear in December 1964 at Albert Draper's scrap yard here in Hull. The other exhibits included the first of the new D49 class, No 234 YORKSHIRE, an equally new Sentinel shunting engine of Y1 class, No 79, and next to it a Y8 0–4–0 tank No 563, built in 1890, which had done all its work on Hull docks. Also on display were class A5 4–6–2T 1712 which worked suburban trains in the Newcastle area, one of the new Sentinel railcars, 212 ECLIPSE, and the shed at Springhead had cleaned and polished one of their newly acquired 2–8–0 powerful goods engines to take part, No 6616. Curiously, no genuine Hull and Barnsley owned engine ever took part in one of these exhibitions.

Hull organised another of these exhibitions on Sunday October 15th 1933 as part of Civic Week, the Sheriff opening it with Major Carver again presiding. Visitors included the Lord Mayor and Lady Mayoress and their guests, the Lord Mayor and Lady Mayoress of London, also 14,129 ordinary citizens, including one of the authors. Nine engines were paraded – the 'Hush–Hush' 10000, 4472 FLYING SCOTSMAN with one of the special corridor tenders, new D49 class 292 THE SOUTHWOLD, B16 1384, Q6 class 2278, A8 2147 just rebuilt from 4–4–4T to a 4–6–2 tank engine, D17 class 1620, Y8 class 563 (again), Sentinel shunter No 174, and although it was not yet LNER–owned, the Diesel–electric railcar LADY HAMILTON. In addition were green and cream painted excursion coaches, buffet and sleeping cars, a camping coach, and the Dairycoates 25–ton breakdown crane.

Starting in 1932 various Education Departments together with the Post Office and LNER railwaymen co–operated to show their work to elementary school children in organised parties, using a locomotive in steam, and a travelling postal van with apparatus for exchanging mail bags. Hull's turn came in April 1934, when for two weeks, engine 736, a C7 4–4–2, was in steam for detailed examination by 2,801 scholars and 112 teachers, from schools in Hull and the East Riding. It had run its normal mileage and was due to go for general repair, so its paint could be trampled upon with impunity. There was an official opening by the Lord Mayor, and Major Carver achieved a hat trick as Chairman, supported by the Divisional General Manager, Directors of Museums and Education and Chairman of the Education Committee were present. There was also the Postmaster, and 100 pupils selected from Hull

Three of the 1928 exhibits, from top to bottom, the Gresley Pacific, Tennant 2–4–0 and new D49 YORKSHIRE.

schools. During the two weeks, D49 class 292 THE SOUTHWOLD was placed in the open air at Paragon station to enable selected students at Hull School of Art to sketch it.

What proved to be the last of these exhibitions for school children took place in Hull and began on Monday April 12th 1937, for two weeks. The cinema coach showed *Pathways of Perfection,* there was the usual Post Office participation, and this time THE SOUTHWOLD was trampled on instead of being the artist's model. The Lord Mayor, and Major Carver did the opening honours, and to the previous VIPs (who all found it worth attending again) were added the Locomotive Running Superintendent from York, the Secretary of the East Riding Education Committee, and the Editor of the *Hull Daily Mail* newspaper.

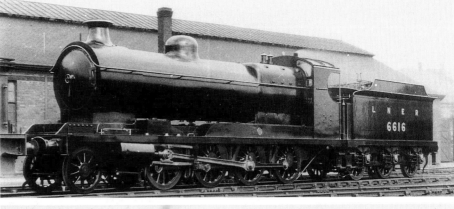

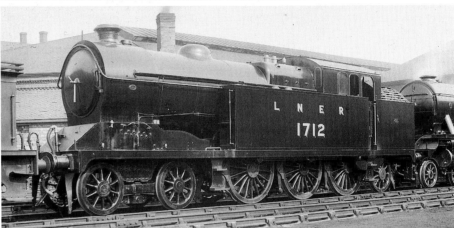

Two more locomotives from the 1928 exhibition, O4 No.6616, A5 No.1712 and bottom, one of the 1933 exhibits No.10000, the Hush–Hush which looked impressive but did not live up to expectations.

CONTINENTAL CONNECTIONS

During the 1939–45 war, as the Allies prepared for the invasion of Europe, Hull Springhead shed began to heed biblical advice, anent 'I was a stranger, and you took me in'. Three illustrations will show just how strange those visitors appeared to eyes accustomed to LNER locomotive lines. USA loco No 2296 was put into British working order by Doncaster works in July 1943 and allocated to Leeds, Neville Hill shed on the 19th of that month. How it got to Springhead shed for shedmaster George Gregory to take its picture remains a wartime secret as he, with proper prudence, did not date his photo. Within three months of our landing in Normandy things were going sufficiently well for 2296 to be shipped abroad. Springhead had regarded the 2–8–0 wheel arrangement as normal for the past fifteen years, but they had certainly not met up with bar frames and double bogie tenders before!

The USA 0–6–0 tank 1938 faced Gregory's camera only after Springhead had cased it up for shipment to France, most likely via Alexandra Dock. Again, he left no evidence as to the date when it visited his shed.

Having never had the slightest inclination to study War Department, or Great Western locomotives, all that can be offered about War Department 199's picture is that the February, 1943 issue of the *Railway Observer* reported that, on 8th January 1943, WD 199, fitted with condensing apparatus, had passed southbound on the GN main line through Welwyn Garden City. So, what it was doing – and when – at Springhead coaling stage baffles me. Note the wartime blackout tarpaulins on the stage, because they were very rarely photographed so clearly.

We now move to connections with the Continent not coming under the heading of 'careless talk,' but still directly connected with Hull's part in the 1939–45 war. Following the defeat of Germany, British troops remained there in considerable numbers for many years, and were known as the British Liberation Army. Arrangements for home leave had to be organised and, starting in October 1945, every day a ship left Cuxhaven for Hull carrying about 1,400 of them. The ships used needed a minimum of 21 feet of water, and so they had to berth in King George Dock, where arrival time was

The strangers from top to bottom, S160 2296, packaged 0–6–0T 1938 and WD 199. The latter probably raised the most eyebrows.

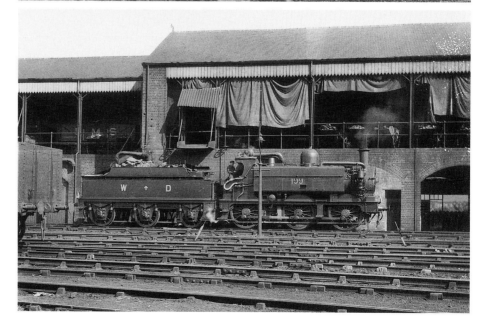

Riverside Quay in 1935 before enemy action took its toll of the facilities.

governed by tide. After the troops disembarked, a fleet of Army lorries took them the three miles to Paragon from where special trains ran, one each to London, Manchester, and Edinburgh. The pre–war Riverside Quay facilities had suffered incendiary bomb damage in May 1941 but of greater importance were the alterations needed to cope with the draught of the ships being used. They were all Liberty ships – EMPIRE RAPIER, EMPIRE CUTLASS, EMPIRE HALBERD and EMPIRE SPEARHEAD. Adequate draught for them, at all states of the tide in the river Humber, was provided through the same device as that used so successfully for the invasion of Normandy, the artificially created Mulberry harbour. The wartime artificial harbour had not needed all the pontoons which had been built to cover possible losses, so two of the spares, still stored on the English side of the Channel, were towed to Hull and moored off Riverside Quay, with gangways connected to it. Using the outer face of the pontoons for berthing, the ships then had a minimum 21 feet of water always available, so regular arrival and departure times could be established.

The berthing of the ships was transferred from King George Dock to the improvised Riverside Quay on 16th August 1946, and the troop trains were then able to leave from tracks which had not been damaged. Facilities were quickly installed allowing entry to the coaches from rail level, and the soldiers reached home much earlier than before. Between October 1945 and the end of 1946, Hull dealt with 120,000 troops each way, and also embarked 38,000 repatriated German prisoners of war.

THOSE INFAMOUS LEVEL CROSSINGS

As already described, by 1869 Hull had lines west to Leeds and Doncaster, north to Beverley, York, and Scarborough, north east to Hornsea, and east to Withernsea. The universally flat terrain, coupled with the railway having become so much more important than the roads – still limited to the speed of a horse – resulted in a gated level crossing on any roads that did have to be crossed. The first of them, Park Street, came within clear sight of the platforms at Paragon station even, and only a quarter mile further came the next, Argyle Street. Incidentally, when these two crossings were made in 1848, they were on what was then known as Pesthouse Lane and Asylum Lane respectively... Every train out of, and in to, Paragon station required the operation of both these crossing gates. Those going west then met level crossings at Anlaby Road, St George's Road, Hawthorn Avenue (then known as Chalk Lane), and Hessle Road, all in the first (or last) two miles of the journey. Trains to Beverley, York, Bridlington, and Scarborough had to deal with Park Street, Argyle Street, the hazard of a right–angle flat rail crossing of the Victoria Dock branch line, and then Walton Street crossing. But Hornsea trains had Park Street, Argyle Street, Botanic Gardens (then known as Cemetery Gates), Park Road (originally Terry Street), Beverley Road (Stepney), Wincolmlee, an opening swing bridge over the river Hull, Chamberlain Road and finally, Tween Dykes Road – all in no more than four miles.

Withernsea trains shared the first six and the river crossing with the Hornsea trains, and then traversed Dansom Lane, Holderness Road, Craven Street, Southcoates Lane and Marfleet crossings, all eleven within the city limits and only five miles from Paragon station. Originally trains on the Victoria Dock branch also had to traverse the level crossing over what is now Cleveland Street. This was abandoned at or about the time of the opening of the new Wilmington station. Chamberlain Road, which was worked by Stoneferry Junction box, was a product of inter–war years housing developments and, as it happened, the last new such installation in the city. There was also, on the Hornsea branch between Wilmington Junction and Stoneferry Junction, Wilmington East signal box. This too had a level crossing, comprising hand worked main gates and wickets.

Though it was only used after 1848 by excursions for passengers, a busy goods line between Hessle Road and Cottingham South junctions added three more level crossings, Haltemprice Street, Anlaby Road (Wheeler Street) and Spring Bank West, which was curiously named Waterworks crossing. That title derived from a siding branching off thereabouts to the Springhead pumping station, built in 1862 to give Hull a water supply from boreholes.

Hedon Road was also crossed on the level by the Victoria Dock branch, and there were a number of un–named crossings with footpath–only access, but 22 road crossings would be both unbelievable, and unacceptable anywhere but in Hull. Starting as early as 1867, some thirty years before the first motor transport even took to the roads, the Council began its badgering of – in turn – the North Eastern, the London & North Eastern, and British Railways about abolishing the level crossings. The sticking point with the North Eastern was usually a decision on how the cost should be apportioned. Hull Council was prepared to pay up to a half but the railway would not go above a third for its share, and it was sitting pretty because there was no legal restriction on the time the gates could be closed in the railway's favour. However, agreement was reached for work to finally start, on Monday 20th February 1871, for the first bridging of a level crossing, that at Park Street, The North Eastern was uncharacteristically cooperative, for it wished to add a couple of platforms to the south side of Paragon station, specifically to deal with excursion, rather than regular traffic, the station itself already being busy enough for the comfort of its normal passengers. So Park Street bridge duly eliminated the first of the crossings, and one which affected every train using Paragon station.

Fifteen years were to pass before another crossing was abolished, and it was February 1887 before Argyle Street (the other one to span all the lines into and out of Paragon station) was bridged.

The first level crossing to be tackled on the eastern side of the city resulted from the opening of Alexandra Dock in 1885. It sparked off property development in the area to the north of the Withernsea line, which in turn led to a need for improved access to the dock. This took the form of an inclined approach from Craven Street and then a 90 degree turn on to a new bridge over the railway line, with an extension of Craven Street on the south side to Hedon Road. Craven Street crossing was thus eliminated in 1893, supplemented by a much improved connection between Holderness and Hedon Roads.

The next level crossing to be abolished was done away with through electrification, and growing road traffic had no influence on it. In 1900 the Corporation applied for an Act of Parliament to run electric tramcars from the city along Hedon Road to Marfleet, and that involved crossing the Victoria Dock branch railway, at right angles on the level. Despite the railway by then being used solely for goods traffic, the House of Lords would not permit such a crossing where electric trams were concerned. In consequence, the railway had to be relaid at a higher level and the Corporation lowered the road under the resulting bridge. Mention has already been made that Hull has an average height above sea level of only some seven feet, and the O.S. bench mark at the bottom of the dip in the

road showed only 3·3 feet. That made flooding almost certain at spring tides, or from exceptional rainfall, and so it proved in later years. However, it was a case of Hobson's choice and the necessary road alteration took until December 1903 before the electric tram service to Marfleet could start. In exchange for the occasional hiccups from flooding, at all other times delays to road traffic had been eliminated by the disappearance of Hedon Road's level crossing.

In 1907 work began on the construction of Hull's largest and most modern dock, which perforce had to be further out on the eastern side of the city. An extensive system of rail lines to service it were provided, but traffic on them would be greatly impeded if it had to negotiate the Southcoates Lane level crossing. So inclines and a bridge (which also spanned the Withernsea line) were built on the eastern side of the existing road and level crossing, to avoid interfering with the existing users. The new bridge came into use on February 25th 1914, in ample time for the opening of the dock by King George the Fifth, which took place 26th June. The King conferred the name of King George Dock upon it, and so one more crossing ceased to operate and cause delays. The 1914–18 war, and the severe trade depression of 1929–32, halted further work at doing away with Hull's level crossings, and only one more went before the 1939–45 war stopped all progress once again.

King George Dock and Alexandra Dock lay to the east of the city, and the increasing road traffic to and from them had to pass through the city centre, a steadily growing burden not only in Hull but on the arterial roads to the west and north. The traffic was a nuisance to city shops and amenities and was considerably impeded by the level crossings on Anlaby, Hessle, and Beverley Roads, leading to growing vexation at the many delays through the railway taking precedence. In the 1930s it was planned to divert much of the road traffic by constructing a ring road around the outskirts of Hull, using some existing roads, and building linking roads where needed. A start was made opposite King George Dock using Marfleet Avenue and the somewhat crooked Marfleet Lane, on which there was a 45 degree level crossing of the Withernsea line, at Marfleet station. Clearly, that had to go, so Marfleet Avenue was extended northwards by a new bridge over the railway. This was ready for use from 12th March 1934, and that level crossing then disappeared. About 2½ miles further on the ring road had to cross the railway line to Hornsea, which was bridged to the same design as that used for Marfleet Avenue. No level crossing was involved there, because the bridge was on a new

section of link road. In dribs and drabs, by March 1934 the Council had thus only managed to get six crossings replaced by bridges, and there was no further progress on abolishing crossings for almost another thirty years.

German bombers having given Hull plenty of scope for rebuilding after the 82 raids on this anonymous 'North–East Coast Town', the Council in 1944 asked Sir Patrick Abercrombie to plan its future. When that was made known, it was regarded as an excellent chance to include the clearance of level crossings. Everybody, including the local newspaper, was taken by surprise to learn that there were as many as sixteen still in active use within the city limits. So, to make its readers aware of them, on 17th October 1944 the *Hull Daily Mail* listed them. They were at Walton Street, Hawthorn Avenue, St George's Road, Haltemprice Street, Spring Bank West (Waterworks), Newington, Botanic Gardens, Park Road, Beverley Road (Stepney), Dansom Lane, Wincolmlee, Holderness Road, Chamberlain Road, Tween Dykes Road, Anlaby Road and Hessle Road.

The Abercrombie Plan was published in 1945, and proposed to deal with the abolition of the level crossings by widening the high level line built by the Hull & Barnsley, also abandoning Paragon station, and building a new terminus near to the existing Cannon Street goods station. No doubt it was a brilliant plan – all it needed for its implementation was money (lots of it) and the requisite powers to push it through. Unfortunately for the Plan, both were not held by the same people, so it had to go on the back burner. The Corporation came up with their own Development Plan in 1951 and that made provision for the removal of five of the sixteen level crossings by bridging at Hessle Road, Anlaby Road, Walton Street, Botanic Gardens, and Stepney (Beverley Road). My researches unearthed a fascinating couple of letters concerning Walton Street crossing. On 30th November 1895, the North Eastern Railway's Solicitor wrote to Hull's Town Clerk pointing out that the Railway's 1896 Parliamentary Bill included the proposed substitution of a bridge for the Walton Street Level Crossing, and asked for the Corporation's views. The Town Clerk replied on 4th December that he had consulted the Chairman of the Works Committee and the Borough Engineer, who both thought 'that the proposed bridge is unnecessary and undesirable, and that it would be a great inconvenience to the public'. The Railway Company were asked to delay seeking any Parliamentary powers for a bridge 'until the Corporation as well as the Company are agreed as to its necessity'. What wonderful opportunity was missed, and almost 100 years later, lines of traffic, cyclists, and pedestrians still fret at the delays, because Walton Street is our most used level crossing. It does also have another item of interest connected with it. On 21st November 1934, the City Council Works Committee minuted that on 31st October 1934 the Ministry of Transport had authorised the use of the traffic lights which had been installed there. It is understood that those were the first of their kind in this country, for controlling a level crossing.

An official survey in 1954 showed that gates at Hessle Road crossing were closed to road traffic on 130 occasions for a total of 6 hours 24 minutes between 7 a.m. and 11 p.m.; at Anlaby Road for 3 hours 40 minutes, and at three other crossings for about 2 hours each.

The Corporation's plans ground forward very slowly, but in 1961 a start was made on the crossing which was the greatest irritant, as revealed by the survey, the one on Hessle Road. A substantial obstacle had first to be removed – the two girder bridges which carried the Hull and Barnsley line to the Neptune Street goods depot over Hessle Road and then the main line railway out to the west. The road traffic flyover became operative on 15th September 1962, which saw the end of the Hessle Road crossing. Attention then turned on to the Anlaby Road crossing; here a longer flyover was required because the road crossed the railway lines at an angle of 45 degrees, but the job was advanced enough for the level crossing to be closed on 31st July 1964.

By then, the Corporation had received some unexpected help with the crossings abolition programme from a Dr. Beeching, who had been responsible for getting both the Hornsea and Withernsea passenger services closed down from 19th October

1964. A goods service to Hornsea continued until 3rd May 1965, but only on a one train a day basis and when that was stopped, the crossings at Chamberlain Road and Tween Dykes Road were abolished. Later that month a new curve joining the Leeds – Doncaster (Victoria Dock) line to the Beverley – Bridlington line was brought into use at a cost of £64,000, of which the city contributed £45,000. This meant that the line from Hessle Road junction to Cottingham south junction could be closed, enabling the crossings at Haltemprice Street, Newington and Spring Bank West (Waterworks) to be abolished from 24th May 1965. So that year saw the closure of no less than six level crossings, and then there was a pause until 1968.

In that year, the money paid to Abercrombie for his Plan 23 years earlier at last brought some tangible return. The goods trains to and from King George Dock, and the timber imports through Victoria Dock still imposed frequent and lengthy delays on two of the main arterial roads, Beverley Road at Stepney, and Holderness Road at Southcoates. They also affected residential traffic on Spring Bank at Botanic Gardens, and industrial traffic on Wincolmlee and on Dansom Lane. Short connections then put in enabled all the docks trains to be switched to the high level line built by the Hull and Barnsley in 1885, just as Abercrombie had recommended. One connection enabled Botanic Gardens, Park Road, Beverley Road (Stepney), and Wincolmlee crossings to be abolished on the 28th October 1968, and the other, on 19th December 1968 did likewise for those at Dansom Lane and Holderness Road – so another six went in that year.

Only four crossings then remained in

operation, as they still do in 1993 (Walton Street is now two completely separate crossings, 'south' on the Paragon side and 'north' for the opposite carriageway), with no known plans for doing away with them. Although the original 22 have been so reduced, those remaining still affect every passenger train into and out of Paragon station. All trains for Leeds and those using the Doncaster line still have to negotiate the crossings at St. George's Road and Hawthorn Avenue, but as neither of these are main roads, they do not unduly handicap road traffic. Technical progress has enabled their warning lights and barriers to be operated from Hessle Road signal box, which monitors them by television. But the profound irony of our Council officials' 1896 refusal of the offer of a bridge to eliminate the Walton Street crossing becomes more pronounced with every year that passes. At the time of the refusal the appreciable amount of land required was readily available, very little of it being occupied by buildings. Now the whole surrounding area is developed and any bridging could only be done at colossal expense. The main road level crossings also posed problems when the street tramways were introduced, special safety features having to be included. There was even a flat crossing of railway lines stemming from as far back as 1853, of the Victoria Dock branch across the 1848 Bridlington line, and which was only dispensed with at the end of 1968. So far as is known, it never caused an accident.

In 1915, the North Eastern Railway did their own bridging to avoid another flat crossing, of the main line out to the west. A new passenger line from Hessle Junction to Hessle Road level crossing was needed because of the extensive Priory mineral yard sidings then being constructed. But instead of proceeding on the level as previously (which would have involved a flat crossing of four lines from the mineral yards to the Dairycoates sidings and to the western docks) an embankment was built to a height of about 20 feet, starting about 1¼ miles from Hessle station, reaching the surface again at Hessle Road level crossing. Over the conflicting lines a single span braced girder bridge, of 179 feet on the skew, carried the passenger lines.

The level crossing and signal box at Southcoates station blend in nicely with all the other premises on Holderness Road in this 1960s view. During the days of steam these gates were the curse of the motorist but now all has been swept away in favour of the motor vehicle. Photograph I.K. Watson.

Walton Street *circa* 1958. When the LNER diverted the H&BR Section passenger trains to Paragon station, it was necessary to provide at Walton Street both a new Junction and signal box. The latter, though basically to the former NER standard 'SD' pattern differed in detail, most obviously (owing to site restrictions) in the 'over–sailing' of the operating floor. An LNER minute of 3rd January 1924 details a contract worth £3,304 8s 0d, let to the Westinghouse Co. for signalling work in connection with a new loop from the H&BR to the NE Hull – Scarborough line, the price including work at Springbank North. Ten years later, during the summer of 1934, the existing gates were converted to power operation and at the same time road traffic lights were installed – the first such application in England. This work too was contracted out to Westinghouse and was authorised by the LNER on 30th November 1933 at a cost of £1,178. Just over eleven months later these later alterations were inspected and approved by the Ministry of Transport, on 31st October 1934. For the next 28 years things were to remain substantially unaltered – until the autumn of 1962, when the level crossing gates were replaced by motor worked 'boom gates' and air–operated wickets. Eventually progress again caught up and from the passing of the last train on Saturday 29th March 1980 Walton Street ceased to be a 'Block Post'. From now on all the signals and points were worked by the Hessle Road signal man, although the gates remained locally worked, from the former signal box. Eventually, on Sunday 19th April 1987 the signal box was demolished and at the same time a new temporary Portakabin brought into use. Change came again on Sunday 9th July 1989, when all the boom gates and wickets were removed, and the first pair of barriers were installed. These were out of use for some time, and when it was necessary to run trains the roadway was roped off. On 16th July the remaining barriers on the north side were installed. Today Walton Street is officially two level crossings – North and South, both worked by closed circuit television (CCTV) from Hessle Road signal box. Walton Street is unique in being the largest level crossing on British Railways. The Leyland bus belongs to East Yorkshire Motor Services and is a Roe–bodied PD2/12 of 1950. Photograph N.E. Stead.

When Priory yard was completed, the reception, empty mineral, and sorting sidings totalled 75 miles, and could accommodate about 11,000 wagons. Concurrently, the expansion of Dairycoates shed and the installation of the mechanical coaling plant was taking place. Further development of Priory inwards yard took place in 1935 with the introduction of hump shunting, similar to that which had proved so successful for the London coal traffic at Whitemoor in Cambridgeshire a few years earlier.

We continue our historical journey now with a more in–depth look at the sites and sights of the railways that once existed within the city boundary.

PARAGON & WEST PARADE

The original 1848 frontage of Paragon station as once seen from Anlaby Road, a mid–1960s view. It remains much the same today, but the little wooden office is long gone.

A mid–Edwardian postcard looking across the new frontage of Paragon. The memorial commemorates local men who fell in the Boer War.

Paragon station looking south west from Ferensway across Collier Street towards the bus station on a very wet and dismal 7th March 1957. The Royal Station Hotel stands to the left of the forecourt.

Looking west from the Paragon Square cenotaph onto the front elevation of the Royal Station Hotel in March 1957.

The Royal Station hotel looking south west March 1957. The advert for Guinness on the shoe shop frontage was for many years a feature of the town centre. At night it was lit up in neon tubes, and then like so many things in life one day it was unnoticed, and it too had gone. Following the 1904 rebuilding of Paragon, the frontage was changed from the south or Anlaby Road side to the Paragon Square or east elevation. The original 1848 entrance was then walled in and used as offices, and remains very much so today. During 1962 the station was again partly rebuilt, and the 1904 frontage was removed, to be replaced by a brick built office block on concrete stilts. This too is now redundant, and is scheduled for demolition.

Paragon looking east from under Park Street Bridge, 1937. There are five locomotives visible, but it is only possible to identify the class of one with any certainty. That is the ex–GN 4-4-2T C12 with its train of clerestory stock over in platform 1. The engine standing at platform 12 has the look of a H&BR tender type, whilst in platform 9 is what appears to be a Hunt or Shire 4–4–0. Prominent are the soon to be removed semaphore signals, and the 1904 Paragon signal box. Like all early power signalling schemes the outside equipment was identical to the contemporary mechanical counterparts, the only difference being in the method of operation. In this case it was by compressed air, instead of wires for the signals, and rodding for the points and bars. This is well illustrated on the right where the points are operated by a separate motor to that of the facing point lock plunger and bar. In the later power schemes the facing point lock plunger was incorporated into the point machine or – putting it simply – in these pioneer schemes the signalman had as many levers to operate as if ordinary mechanical means were employed. The signalman was of course relieved of the strain of manipulating heavy levers, and now needed little more than finger power. Note that the outgoing 'Calling On' signal arms have rings, this was for some reason unique to Hull Paragon. The NER never used them elsewhere on any mechanical or power installations. Space considerations would be important when deciding to use power or mechanically worked points and signals. For example Paragon signal box was 36ft. by 12ft. inside, and yet contained 143 levers. In contrast Staddlethorpe Junction box (now Gilberdyke) is exactly the same size inside, but contains an interlocking frame of only 55 mechanical levers. Similarly, in a cramped station layout such as Paragon it would be very difficult to arrange the necessary 'runs' for the mass of wires and rods associated with mechanical signalling.

The taxi offices on Ferensway with some nice period motor vehicles and advertising in March 1957.

Looking across Paragon concourse in the mid–1960s, a typical mixture of the old and new – original NER seats, LNER style platform numbers, penny number–tag stamper, and the plastic 1960s milk machine. Photograph Ian K. Watson.

One of the last survivors of class D20, No.62396, heads a stopping passenger train out of Hull Paragon on 29th June 1957. It is minus its shed plate, but when withdrawn some five months later the engine had moved north to Alnmouth.

J39 No.64914 stands in one of the long excursion platforms, No.13, during 1959. 37 was probably a Paragon pilot and would shunt the station and Walton Street carriage sheds.

A nice panoramic view of Paragon yard and station on 29th April 1963, taken from Park Street bridge and not a steam locomotive in sight. Photograph I.K. Watson.

Sandwiched between two Cravens diesel multiple units, class A1 Pacific No.60140 BAL-MORAL, draws an E.C.S train out of Hull Paragon. 60140 was subsequently to pay at least one more visit to Hull and four years later made that inevitable one way journey to Drapers at Sculcoates, to be cut up on 7th April 1965. In all ten of these magnificent

Looking for all the world like a well stocked model railway is Paragon Yard just before noon on Saturday 4th October 1952. As long ago as the 1904 rebuilding Paragon had been at the forefront of signalling technology. First with the electro – pneumatic worked points and semaphores, and then from 1938 with its route relay interlocking and colour light signals. Conversely, word of that so–useful modern invention electricity had yet to spread to those responsible for providing the yard and platform illumination. The humble gas light was obviously still considered suitable, and continued to serve right up to the dawn of the swinging 'sixties. From left to right the first loco is ex–Great Northern C12 4–4–2T No.67397 on the 12.08 p.m. Saturdays only to Withernsea, standing in platform 2. Next is an unidentified ex–North Eastern G5 0–4–4T backing into platform 4 to couple on to the stock of the 12.12 p.m. Saturdays only to South Howden. An unknown B1 4–6–0 comes next, standing at the head of the 12.10 p.m. Leeds train in platform 6. Backing into platform 8 to couple up to the 12.5 p.m. Kings Cross train is B1 No.61168 of Mexborough shed, which will take that train as far as Doncaster. Behind the water crane is class A5 No.69811, setting the stock for a Boothferry Park football special into the excursion platform No.13. There are, on close inspection, some two dozen coaches visible, most of them stored alongside the station in the North sidings. Today this scene, if it were possible to recreate it, would (apart from the Kings Cross HST) be wholly dominated by the two car DMU. The South Howden and Hornsea services are of course long gone, and just a distant memory. Officially Boothferry Park station is still available for the football trains, but it is now many years since it was in use. North Sidings were lifted quite some years ago, and now in the closing years of the second millennium a loco hauled train is a very rare sight. Indeed some would consider two dozen coaches in Paragon within twelve months to be a very good year.

J94 No.68011 sorts out some fish vans at Paragon in 1958. This traffic has long gone from the railway; indeed the vast trawler fleet which was once based in Hull is now but a shadow of its former self.

Class V3 No.67684 stands bunker first in platform 9 waiting to depart with the 4.20 pm Hull – Brough stopper. It will return from Brough at 5.15, stopping at all stations and loaded to capacity with workers from Blackburns aircraft factory. As late as this, 22nd August 1963, apart from the rolling stock the station – including the gas lights – had changed little from its rebuilding almost 60 years before.

On the 22nd August 1958 D49 No.62741 THE BLANKNEY stands in platform 4 waiting for the right away. Coming alongside Gresley 2–6–2T No.67684 brings an interesting mix of various LNER and BR standard type empty coaches, probably from the nearby Walton Street carriage sidings. Also of interest, little more than a year after its introduction, all of the coaches are in the later maroon livery.

D49 No.62710 LINCOLNSHIRE sets back with a very mixed assortment of wagons into platform 12. The presence of a cattle wagon is unusual, but the vans would be used for any parcels traffic, which was then of course quite prolific. Marshalled in the middle is an ex–LMS 6 wheel 'Stove' or BGZ. A standard MK1 coach stands between 12 and 13 platforms in the appropriately named middle sidings, whilst to the left in platform 11 is an LNER Thompson designed 'match board' full brake. Photograph I.K. Watson

With Class V3 2–6–2T No.67640 of Dairycoates shed in charge, the Hull portion of the 'Yorkshire Pullman' waits to depart from Platform 8 at Paragon. Working the train as far as Doncaster, the V3 will come off there so that the Hull section can be attached to the main portion of the train from Leeds, and then conveyed on to Kings Cross. On the far left can be seen the buffet car of one of the then recently introduced Trans Pennine diesel units. Apart from this, and the round platform numerals which were an LNER addition, the scene has changed very little since the 1904 rebuilding of the station. Photograph N.E. Stead.

An unusually clean 61165 of Canklow makes a smoky start as it draws away with a short express from Paragon's platform 11. Over in platform 1 another express is about to depart with a K3 2–6–0 at its head. This carries the more usual livery of the period – plain dirt.

A comparatively rare interior view of the 1904 Paragon signal box. The lever frame was of the McKenzie & Holland type 'B' pattern and controlled all signals, points and bars, electro-pneumatically, despite being contained in a box only 36 feet by 12 feet inside. The train signalling instruments on the block shelf above the levers are as used elsewhere on the NER. Indeed the block bells are of a style still locally in use today, and up to recent times examples of the 'Block telephone' remained. Likewise the Block instruments in a modified form still continue to signal trains safely. At the time of its installation, the signalling was amongst the most modern in the world – yet the box was gas lit!

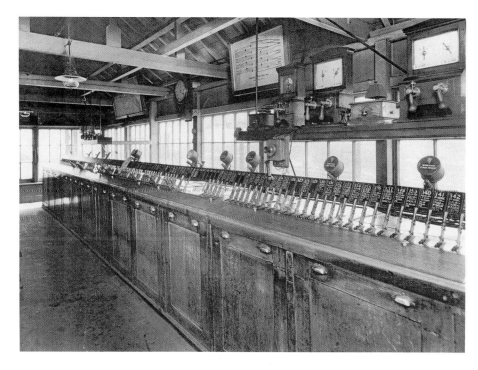

Leeds Holbeck based A3 No.60088 BOOK LAW has a crowd of schoolboy spotters admiring its graceful lines before its 4.00 pm departure to Leeds with the Liverpool train in 1960. One could travel to Liverpool and Manchester by three different routes during this period either via the old Great Central line through Sheffield; over the L&Y route or by the route this train will take over the former London & North Western. Just a few years after this scene was captured some specially built diesel multiple units, complete with buffet cars and christened 'Trans–Pennine' trains, took over the service using the ex–LNWR line from Leeds westwards. That same route is the only survivor today and below we see one of the 'Trans–Pennine' units at Paragon nearing the end of its career in 1984.

The cylinder taps on K3 61846 are slammed shut as the 12.20 p.m. Kings Cross is started from Hull Paragon on 22nd January, 1962. Photograph Peter Rose.

Looking west from 2 and 3 platform ends at Paragon, in October 1956, towards West Parade Junction. Prominent under Park Street bridge is the new signal box of 1938. This still remains in use today but on December 2nd 1984 the original O.C.S. panel was replaced by one of the modern 'entrance–exit' patterns. However all was not lost, and the 1938 panel was sent to the National Railway Museum at York for eventual restoration. During the last war the signal box suffered at least one near miss, and although the building was damaged all the equipment continued to work. This was of course much to the pride of Westinghouse, the original makers and installers. It is not generally known but at first it was the LNER's intention to retain the semaphores – the LNER Traffic Committee meeting of 28th March 1935 for instance recommended "...the modernization of Hull Paragon and Park St. signalling arrangements, the signal boxes to be amalgamated and provision of a new signal box. Tenders to be invited, estimated cost £25,773". Only on 28th May 1936 were colour lights recommended 'and not semaphores', the Westinghouse tender to be accepted at a cost of £28,985.

Paragon Yard, 3rd October 1956, looking east through the arches of Park Street bridge. This was once a level crossing but was replaced very early. The siding on the left leads to the Civil Engineer's store yard, and some of their equipment is seen stored on the loading dock. Through the middle arch are the lines leading to North sidings, the loading dock and platforms 1, 2 and 3. Centre is the base of the 1904 Paragon signal box, now stripped of its operating floor and used as a shunter's lobby. On the extreme right is one support leg of the signal bridge so prominent in the May 1937 picture. An A5 4–6–2T stands on platform 3 ready to depart probably for Hornsea or Withernsea. This was the last full year of complete steam working from Paragon and evidence of the many empty or spare sets required can be seen stood in the excursion platforms, under the main bridge span. The platforms are still lit by gas, and would remain so for some years yet. As long ago as July 1930 *The Railway Magazine* quoted: *"The station is rather old fashioned, in that it is still lighted by gas. A very good standard of illumination is however realised. Indeed at one time Paragon station was regarded as one of the best applications of the system employed, that of the British Gas Lighting Co Ltd. The station has its own generating plant".*

West Parade from Argyle Street Bridge 19th April 1963. A four car DMU heads past West Parade signal box with an up Scarborough branch train bound for Paragon. In the middle distance can be seen Walton Street carriage sheds. Between these and the railwayman's cottage run the lines of the goods only Victoria dock branch. These cross the Scarborough lines on the level by means of a 90 degree crossing, an unusual feature illustrated elsewhere in this album. Going away sharply to the right are the Up and Down Withernsea branch. These join the Victoria Dock branch at Botanic Gardens some 849 yards distant. Joining the Down Withernsea line is the connection to Botanic Gardens shed by then used solely by DMU's. Incidentally the semaphore signal above the train was the last example to signal trains on a passenger carrying line in the city. It was first brought into use on 20th December 1953, and remained in use until 29th March 1980 when at 11.20 p.m. West Parade box was abolished. Photograph I.K. Watson.

The worst accident in local railway history occurred on the approach to Paragon station just east of the Argyle Street bridge, at about 9.10 am on 14th February 1927. An incoming Withernsea train was in head–on collision with the 9.5 am departure to Scarborough. Both trains were drawn by 4–4–0 type engines, No.96 of class D22 on the Withernsea train, and class D17 No.1628 bound for Scarborough. The resulting damage was of such a catastrophic nature that both locomotives were withdrawn and cut up. Initially eight lives were claimed and a further four subsequently died in hospital. 24 passengers suffered serious injury, and the crews also. The collision occurred directly behind what is now the Hull Royal Infirmary, and to help in the swift removal of the injured, part of the hospital wall was knocked down.

Sometime about 1957 what had been 'A' line between West Parade and Paragon was dispensed with for traffic purposes. The connection was taken out at West Parade, after which the trackwork was partly relined, and a purpose–built twin carriage washing machine provided. At first this was manually operated, and in this view of 18th April 1963, the operator can be seen in his control tower. Passing through the 'Washer' as it was referred to by the local carriage cleaning gang is a Cravens DMU, which under TOPs would later become Class 105. Photograph I.K. Watson.

It is often said that the North Eastern Railway was the most elaborately signalled in the country, though perhaps in many ways this is open to conjecture. At most of the larger installations the signalling was no more nor no less complex than on any other of the old companies. By the early years of the present century semaphore signalling was at its zenith, and like any other large railway centre Hull had its noteworthy examples. Typical of the period is the magnificent display that once could be seen on the approach to Hull Paragon at Westparade Junction. This is the structure on 6th May 1937; it was first erected in 1904 and came fully into use during 1905, with a total of 22 arms spanning four tracks. From left to right are:- 107 E line to Up Main Home – 19 Anlaby Road distant below; 108 E line to Down Scarborough Home – 20 Victoria Crossing Outer distant below; 109 E line to Down Withern-sea Home – 38 Botanic Gardens distant below; 43 Shunting E line to engine shed; 28 D line to F line Starting – (30) Park Street distant below; 27 D line Starting – (22) Park Street distant below; 97 C line to Up Main Home – 19 Anlaby Road distant below; 101 C line to Down Scarborough Home – 20 Victoria Crossing Outer distant below; 105 C line to Down Withern-sea Home – 38 Botanic Gardens distant below; 42 Shunting C line to engine shed; 25 B line Starting – (10) Park Street distant below; 24 B line to A line Starting – (1) Park Street distant below. Apart from the repainting of the distant signal arms to the now familiar yellow, the entire structure is much as when first put up some 33 years previously. The most noticeable difference are the ingoing Park Street distants; all of these now have their arms permanently fixed at caution, and additionally the D and F line arms also have the green spectacle glasses removed. Owing either to the close proximity of the road bridge obstructing the view, or the distance from the controlling signal box, most of the signal arms are electrically repeated in

the respective signal box. The mechanical linkage and the circuit breakers are visible above the arms so fitted. Towards the bottom of each doll are the wood storage boxes for the necessary batteries. Apart from the addition of two upper quadrant 'Calling On' arms on 25th April 1938, and the later removal of the two Victoria Crossing box Outer Distants in July 1945, the entire signal bridge was to remain much the same for a further fifteen years. On Sunday 20th December 1953, in connection with an extensive resignalling scheme, ten of the remaining signal arms were removed, leaving just 12 arms in use. All were still lower quad-rant, and all originated from the 1904/5 resignalling. Seven months and one week later, on Sunday 25th July 1954, the modernization scheme was completed. When new colour light signals were commissioned, the remaining remnants were taken out of use and soon re-moved. At ground level there is much of interest, especially to the railway modeller. On the left with its straight switch blade is the Engine Siding trap point No.89. This is protected by a McKenzie & Holland rotating ground signal, No.88, a product of the last century but still being installed until around 1937, when the disc signal (which is still today a familiar sight) superseded it. Two fogmans' huts are visible; the nearer one is sited between C and D lines, but actually 'Fogs' the outgoing E line. The fogging machine is in the 'six foot' between E and D lines while its single operating lever is just outside the hut. Part of Victoria Crossing signal box is just discernible through the first brick arch – this is the only known photograph of this box. Numbers in this caption refer to the relevant lever numbers in the controlling signal box. Numbers in brackets viz – 30, 22, 10, 1, are the former lever numbers signal arms, now fixed. The scene of the February 14th 1927 collision, incidentally, was midway between the Argyle Street road bridge, and the large bridge of signals.

Signals at Paragon, 6th May 1937. This is an LNER publicity shot taken in connection with the 1938 Route Relay Interlocking and colour light signalling scheme. The building under construction on the left is the new panel signal box, brought into use just over eleven months later on April 24th 1938. When the NER rebuilt Paragon station in 1904 they chose to power–work the new signals and built two new boxes, 'Paragon' and 'Park Street'. These were both fitted with miniature lever frames of the Westinghouse style 'B', and all of the outside equipment and the interlocking frames were supplied by the company's usual contractor McKenzie & Holland. Almost identical installations had already been installed in the New-castle area. Unlike the northern scheme, however, Annetts Route Indicators were employed, and therefore the Paragon installation did not have the great forest of direction signals. Four of these indicators are visible in this picture – their use saved something like an additional fifteen signal arms and dolls. For some reason the NER did not take up the use of route

indicators of any form and the Paragon installation remained unique. Also relatively unusual for the NER is the practice seen on the right – mounting direction signals one above the other on a common post. The nearer of the two signal bridges survived the 1938 alterations and, fitted with colour light signals, remained in use until the mid–1970s. Shunting in the back-ground is a former H&BR 0–6–0, among the last of that company's tender engines to remain in service. Prior to the 1938 resignalling the 230 possible routes were controlled by a total of 322 miniature levers. When the colour light signals and new box were brought into use there was no alteration to the permanent way. Indeed such was the quality of the original equip-ment that many of the existing point machines were retained and, suitably modified, conti-nued to be worked from the new panel. Although not visible in this view, when first brought into use, the Calling On signals had ringed arms. This was unique and not repeated else-where.

PARAGON TO MARFLEET & BRANCHES

69796 was first built by the NER as a 4–6–0T in March 1908, originally intended for work on the coast line from Scarborough to Whitby. The class soon became referred to as 'Whitby Willies'. Over the years several migrated to Botanic Gardens and occasionally Dairycoates; No.69796 was to become the final member of the class and was withdrawn in March 1953 after having spent the last 18 months of its life as the Paragon carriage pilot.

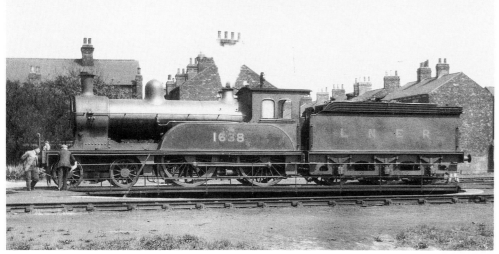

Originally NER Class M1, built Gateshead works in December 1893, No.1638, now LNER class D17, is being turned at Botanic shed. Although withdrawn as long ago as November 1937 sister engine No.1621, restored to its full NER livery, lives on in the National Railway Museum for all to admire.

About the time of this picture Botanic Gardens could boast an allocation of six of these big 'Pacific tanks'. No.69858 of class A8 is seen in the shed yard on 10th July 1956. The great influx of diesel railcars in the late 1950s soon saw them off, and by the mid–summer of 1960 the entire class had passed into history.

Botanic Gardens shed in November 1955 with the centre section of roof already taken down ready for demolition and rebuilding. A typical North Eastern roundhouse, the shed contained two 50ft turntables which were taken out after the shed was rebuilt so that conversion to diesel operation could be carried out. A third 50ft turntable had been provided by the NER outside in the yard at the south end of the shed for turning other companies engines; that turntable is still in existence today and is used to turn diesel railcars when necessary.

When No.292, the Hunt variant of the Gresley D49 4–4–0, fitted with Rotary Cam Lentz poppet valves arrived at Botanic shed in August 1933, it was the first new engine to be allocated there for ten years. For long the Shires and Hunts were a common sight in Hull and by the outbreak of the last war there were fifteen members of the class working from Botanic Gardens, plus of course others working in from surrounding sheds. THE SOUTHWOLD eventually moved away and subsequently, as 62748, withdrawn from Neville Hill in December 1957.

41

The former Great Central 'Director' 4–4–0's of LNER class D11 were fairly rare visitors to Hull. Having worked in from Sheffield, on a train originating from Liverpool, No.5501 MONS makes its way for servicing.

With its tender already coaled up for the return trip, Edge Hill Jubilee 45681 ABOUKIR rests in Botanic Gardens shed yard. The reporting number W611 suggests the engine has worked in a special from the Western Division of the LM Region. Apart from this all that is known is the date, sometime in March 1957. Alongside is Botanic Gardens B1 61215 WILLIAM HENTON CARVER, ('Old Bill' as one of the authors called the B1 when he was a youthful train spotter) was later transferred to Dairycoates, and for many years after could be seen on local trips. All came to an end with withdrawal in March 1965, and cutting up at Drapers yard two months later on 19th May. Although twenty years separate this picture and that of Dreadnaught 10464, it's interesting to note the identical style of the train reporting numbers.

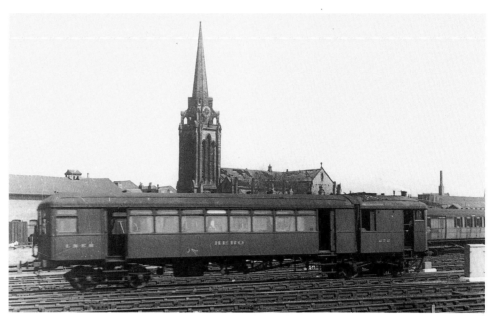

Sentinel steam railcar No.272 HERO makes its way into Paragon on a local service in May 1946. In the background St Stephen's church still bears the scars of war, its roof almost devoid of slates. Photograph H.C.Casserley.

Botanic Gardens station was just one mile out from Hull Paragon, and until Saturday 17th October 1964 served the branch trains to Hornsea and Withernsea. The station post–dates the opening of the Victoria Dock branch and here, like at Anlaby Road, passengers were originally set down or picked up on the level crossing. Previously known as Cemetery Gates, from 1st November 1881 the station was given the more upmarket name of Botanic Gardens. This derived from the nearby, but now long–defunct, pleasure gardens (Hymers College was built on the dite in 1893). Ironically, well over 100 years later the cemetery still exists. To meet the needs of the ever–increasing local population, during 1891 a small coal yard was established. It was situated on the Down side and, behind the one and only station building, it is invisible in this view. The new connection, along with the associated signalling, was inspected by the Board of Trade on December 5th 1891. Destined to out–live the passenger service by 2½ years, they were not officially taken out of use until Monday 24th April 1967. Even so, through trains continued to use this part of the branch for a further 18 months, until 28th October 1968, when traffic was diverted via the high level H&BR route. Eventually, after standing derelict for many years the station was demolished in the mid–1970s.

Park Road gate box was on the Victoria Dock branch not quite midway between Stepney and Botanic stations. Seen here in 1965, it was first opened during the early years of this century when it was known as Terry Street. From 15th June 1943 the gate box ceased to work the signals, these becoming the sole province of Stepney signal box. It survived to control the gates only until this part of the line closed on October 28th 1968. Reproduced by kind permission N. Fleetwood.

Footbridges have always been a popular vantage point for railway photographers, and as this mid–1960s view well illustrates Stepney was no exception. By this date the Hornsea & Withernsea branch trains had gone, and were no more than a pleasant memory of a childhood trip to the seaside. Similarly, with the demise of the railway as a common carrier the goods yard and its reception loop is closed and lifted. These had been entered via the facing slip points seen rusting away in the centre of the picture, and to use that delightful expression so common in the official weekly notices of the period "Spiked out of use pending removal". Although goods facilities had existed from the earliest days the direct facing connection was not brought into use until 1903. In the background the line is crossed by the H&BR bowstring girder bridge, which at this date still carried the long--singled Cannon Street branch. The signal box, the second one to bear the Stepney name is, apart from the bay window, a standard S1 type, and is unworthy of further comment. Across the line is the one–time gateman's hut, which along with its occupant became surplus to requirements some years before. This was from about 1960, when the early 'Wig Wag' version of the present day flashing light road signals were first introduced. One of these can be seen on the extreme left alongside the safety barrier. Close observation of the main gate also reveals that in addition to the large oil lamp, small electric lights are fitted under the gate top rail. Today, apart from the *Station Hotel* on the extreme left, which still dispenses fine beer, nothing of this scene remains.

The only major engineering work on the 3¼ mile Victoria Dock branch was the Sculcoates swing bridge over the river Hull. By 1st June 1864, apart from the bridge itself the entire line had been doubled. To save the expense of a new bridge, and also to simplify train working, the extra line was interlaced alongside the old. With the coming of the new century and a vast increase in rail traffic the original bridge was rapidly becoming something of a bottleneck. By 12th August 1902 plans were being prepared to divert the railway slightly north and build a new double line bridge. Even so there seems to have been no sense of urgency, and over three years were to elapse before the contract with Messrs. Harman & Langton, Engineers, was signed on 29th October 1905. Work must have been quickly put in hand, and by 16th July 1906 the sinking of the centre caisson was under way. Construction proceeded at a rapid pace and by 7th September this was completed and the centre bearing casting was in place. Looking west across the river Hull, the railway company's Sculcoates goods station forms the background. This became a casualty of the Beeching era, but still stands today, having listed building status. Currently there are plans to turn it into a garden centre.

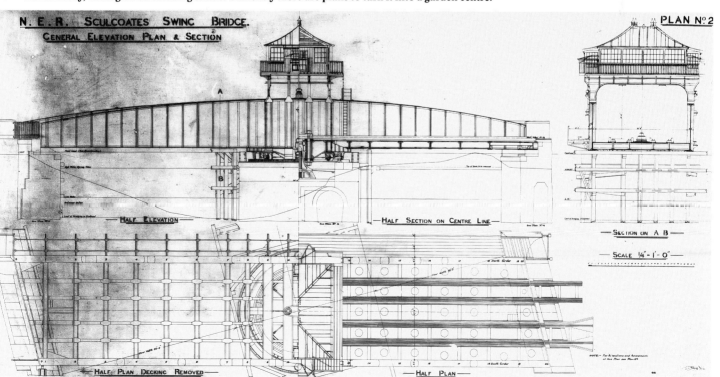

View westward during the early days of the construction of the new double line bridge. By present day standards the machinery available to the workforce is somewhat primitive. Towards the centre of this view two workmen with a hand powered crane prepare to lift a portion of the bridge caisson off a flat wagon. To the right meanwhile, standing ready with his bucket of mortar, the steam crane driver looks on. Towards the right foreground, complete with its vertical boiler and steam engine, is a rail mounted pile driver. An identical machine can also be seen behind the steam crane. On the extreme right and supported by timber baulks is the embryo platework that will eventually form the north girder of the new bridge. The original single line span of 1853, seen on the left of this view, shows off well the interlaced track. Behind are the level crossing gates, a typical NER cast iron footbridge, and in the far distance the H&BR bow string girder bridge. The signal with its arm and spectacle glasses at different levels, and *sans* finial was probably home made by the NER.

18 APR 1907

An inside view of the bridge control room taken just four days prior to the crossing of the first train on May 10th 1907. The fact that work is as yet incomplete is apparent at the lower left, and is borne out by the chisel and wood shavings left by some long forgotten craftsman. Behind the bridge machinery, is an ordinary McKenzie & Holland 'No 16 apparatus' lever frame, which by this date was the standard pattern of interlocking frame for all new works on the NER. The swingbridge was not 'A Block Post' and therefore, unlike a signal box, did not accept trains. Here the bridge man opened and closed it as necessary, and so allowed the passing of river traffic. As at other, similar, locations shipping had priority over the railway. Above the levers and from left to right on the instrument shelf are, Signal Repeater, Sykes Lock & Block instrument, closing switch and, for communication with the nearby signalman at Sculcoates Junction, an ordinary block bell. Lock & Block was not normally used for train signalling on the NER, but was provided at some swing bridges to afford extra protection. Behind the levers and coming from the Sykes instrument are the down rods which controlled the mechanical lever locks. The wording on the instrument reads: ALL LEVERS – LOCKED /–/ STATION BOX – UNLOCKED and indicates the swing bridge to be in position and correctly bolted and locked for the passage of trains. Conversely with the bridge released to pass river traffic the instrument would display: ALL LEVERS – UNLOCKED /–/ STATION BOX – LOCKED. Behind the lever frame, furthermore, is a mechanically worked 'Lock Indicator' and this too was a product of the railway signal engineers McKenzie & Holland of Worcester. Incidentally, by this period M&H had established themselves as almost exclusive contractors to the NER. Of the five levers in the locking frame only three are in use, their purpose being – No.1 Release, No.2 Disengagers, No.3 Latches; the remaining two levers, 4 and 5, are spare. Other points of interest are the (then) relative luxury of electric lighting, and the wall mounted telephone with its separate earpiece and external bell. Today, the latter, which is in all certainty a direct line to Sculcoates signal box, would be much sought after by collectors of the early 'Speaking instrument' (Around this period the term 'Speaking instrument' was much used in official railway publications, in lieu of the present 'telephone').

Our intrepid lensman was evidently made of stern stuff; to obtain this near–birdseye view he lugged the heavy camera and glass plates up to a dizzy height. Nevertheless at high water on that long ago Thursday that was 18th April 1907 he recorded for posterity a powerful vision of things past. The differing stature of the two bridges, with the new completely surpassing that of the old is shown to advantage. During the three week period which elapsed between rolling the new structure into place and its ultimate commissioning on May 10th there must have been considerable disruption. Clearly, and owing to their close proximity, it is now impossible to swing either bridge, and north of Sculcoates the river is all but barred to navigation. Similarly on the west bank that close–by, but delightfully named street 'Wincolmlee' was also closed from time to time.

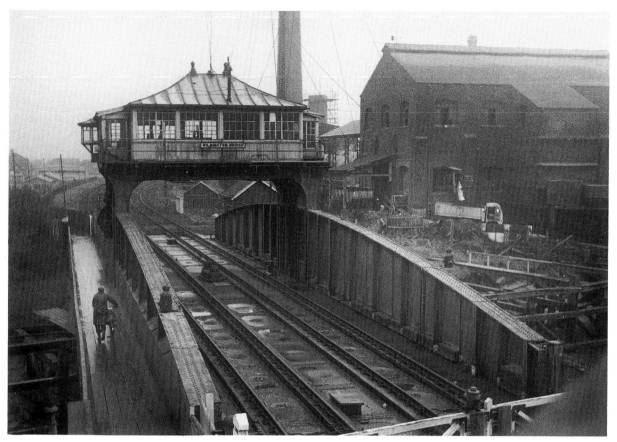

Renamed Wilmington Bridge at some time in the past, this was Sculcoates bridge sixty years on during a wet January in 1967. Photograph Peter Rose.

(opposite top) Looking east three days before being commissioned. The dismantling of the original bridge is now well underway and rails have been stripped from the span, itself liberated from the centre bearing and drawn back, to stand on solid ground.

(opposite bottom) An obviously posed picture taken on Saturday 11th May 1907, the first full working day of the new bridge. A group of children have gathered on the west bank, and eagerly await the attention of the photographer. Behind is the now redundant fixed span of the original 1853 bridge.

Wilmington swing bridge survives as the property of Hull Corporation. Some years ago the drive mechanism and the control system was thoroughly overhauled and brought up to date although much of the NER equipment survives. Outwardly things, even down to the restored livery, are much the same as intended in 1907 except for the outside footpath which has been moved onto the main span of the bridge. The access stairway is a modern intervention, previously a ladder had sufficed. When the NER obtained its Act of Parliament to build this new bridge, it was stipulated that a public footpath be provided. If it was not for this, one can safely presume the bridge, like the Victoria Dock branch, would have gone long ago.

This picture is worthy of inclusion, if only because Chamberlain Road was the last of the many level crossings to be constructed in the city. When first brought into use during 1913 Stone Ferry Junction signal box controlled only the connections and associated signals of the new Stone Ferry goods branch. Though not visible here, it deviated away from the Hornsea branch in a more or less northwesterly direction, its ultimate destination being the premises of the Premier Oil and Cake Mills Ltd, some 1,163 yards off. The branch with its 20 m.p.h. speed restriction was worked by the 'One Engine in Steam' regulations and the train staff for this when not on the engine was kept in the signal box. The new works and signal box were examined by the Board of Trade Inspector on 23rd January 1914, and his report makes reference only to an interlocking frame of 25 levers. At this date there was no level crossing – this came later with the development of the many inter–war housing schemes. The signal box outlived the Hornsea branch passenger service by two weeks, officially closing from Sunday November 1st 1964. This view probably dates from the winter of 1964/65, with the gates and signal box still substantially intact. The window panes will have been stripped out by the locking fitter to ease the task for him and his mate when dismantling the interlocking frame. Redundant signal box windows were much sought after by the local railwaymen, for use as cold frames or greenhouses in their gardens. Photograph I.K. Watson

Deep in the industrial heartland of east Hull, Dansom Lane was crossed by the Victoria Dock branch. Up to the 1960s railways and level crossings were all part of everyday life. The view illustrates well how the railway blended with the landscape. Originally the gates were worked by a crossing keeper, and it was not until the early months of 1904 that a signal box was provided. When inspected by the Board of Trade on 18th April 1904 this contained a frame of 31 levers of which 19 were in use. Apart from working the level crossing gates the signalman also had control over the new and altered connections to Wilmington Goods. This design of box was shortlived and almost exclusive to the Hull Engineers Dept. Photograph I.K. Watson.

Of the original Victoria Dock branch signal cabins only Southcoates survived until the end, and then in a modified and rebuilt form. Although the exact date is unknown the building has its origins in about 1875, and the introduction of block working. Certainly by 1st November 1877, and the publication of the first NER Appendix, a signal box existed here. What now remains of the early NER signalling records suggests that as built the box measured 23ft.6in. by 13ft.6in. inside, with the operating floor 9 feet above rail height. About this period an interlocking frame of 30 levers was in use plus a further 2 levers and 2 gate wheels. Like its contemporaries at Paragon and Anlaby Road etc. Southcoates was built with splay corners and a hipped roof. About the turn of the century Southcoates became quite an important local rail centre. To cope with the ever increasing traffic the signal box was increased in length by a couple of feet and in width by as much as 6ft.6in. Two separate lever frames were now provided – the main line frame, lever Nos.1–34 with 29 working levers and the shunting frame lever Nos.35-74 of which 29 levers were in use. Additionally the gates were worked by a wheel, and there was also the tram signal and catchpoint lever frame. Like elsewhere in the city the bay window was provided to give the signalman a better view of the approaching tramcars. Over 90 years on, and with the usual benefit of hindsight it is hard to appreciate why the humble electric tram needed such elaborate protection. That is until one realises that prior to their introduction the fastest vehicle on the road had been the horse and cart. Rather unusually, in the rebuilding the rear elevation has acquired a complete set of fully glazed windows (see page 20). By the date of this picture the box would be somewhere around 90 years old. Subsidence has set in, and the whole of the upper woodwork is starting to lean backwards. The adverts are from the early British Rail logo period, the one on the left telling all of the virtues of the freightliner service. On the extreme right we learn of a weekend in London including rail fare for a mere £7 17s 6d. Cheap by the standards of today, but almost three decades ago this was more than half a week's wages. Photograph I.K. Watson.

Unidentified English Electric Type 3 with oil tanks ex–Saltend passing through the closed Southcoates Station. 8J01 was a control orders pilot so the precise details of the train working are unknown. When this picture was taken the signal bridge had only recently been removed.

(opposite top) It was somewhat unusual for either Botanic or Dairycoates sheds to be allocated a new engine, but to prove the exception J39 No.1509 was sent ex–works to the latter shed on 25th January 1938. When caught at Southcoates by the camera on 14th May of that year 1509 was less than four months old. The train had first departed Paragon at 5.25 p.m. and stopping only at Southcoates was booked to arrive at Withernsea 38 minutes later. After a layover of 44 minutes the engine and stock then worked back to Hull stopping at all stations. On the return trip a further eleven minutes was alloted for the additional nine station stops. The engine was one of several batches, home made by the LNER at their Darlington works. In all she gave almost 27 years service, and as No.64934 was among the last of its class to be withdrawn, during December 1962. Above the engine is a typical McKenzie & Holland 'iron signal bridge'; this will be *circa* 1904 vintage, but by now has an interesting mix of both upper and lower quadrant signals. This in a slightly rationalized form was to outlive the engine by a few years and was not replaced until the mid–1960s.

(opposite bottom) The original Southcoates station was situated to the bottom right of this picture, approximately between the coal yard and the buffer stop. During the last century it was taken out of use and new island platform and buildings provided. These can be seen towards the left with the Withernsea branch lines on either side. Both old and new stations are shown on an NER plan of September 1894, but the later station is now bereft of platforms. In the centre are the maze of sidings, reception and goods only lines; the latter will eventually reach King George Dock, via Southcoates Lane, Sweet Dews and Holderness Drain North. Leading off to the right and beyond is the branch to Victoria Dock via Drypool. The importance of the timber trade to the area is well illustrated, and visible on the skyline are at least two saw mills and, stacked on the extreme left in 'Soccy Yard' is ample evidence of the finished product. The lines in the foreground are, from left to right: Down & Up main, engine siding, shunt neck and coal siding. Also prominent, but seen here from the reverse side is the Up main starting signal, with Dansom Lane's distant below.

Whilst their drivers and firemen enjoy a well earned midday break, five ex–NER 0–6–0Ts await their return. The engines are from left to right: J71 68230 (the first of its class in the BR series – some had been withdrawn pre–war); J72s Nos.68753, 68718, 68751; J71 68232. This was a typical lunchtime scene at Drypool, caught here 12th September 1956. Of interest to railway modellers are the very short switches, the retention of the old style 'Goose Neck' stretcher bars, and the general rough condition of the permanent way. Photograph N.E. Stead.

The Sentinel 0–4–0 engines with their short wheelbase were ideal for shunting on the tight curves of the Victoria dock. Eight years after nationalisation Y3 8183 still sports its LNER number on the buffer beam. On the right is a standard agricultural tractor modified for railway shunting, by the provision of the steel buffing plates at each end. Known locally as 'Tow motors', they were first introduced in the early 1920s, and could be seen elsewhere in the city. They went out of use quite some years ago, but right up to the mid–1980s an example could be seen shunting the yard at Beverley, eight miles away.

Lines of timber bogies seen at Victoria Dock on 12th January 1967. In use, these would be loaded with the same kind of sawn timber seen in the wagons behind, and when towed between ship and storeyard by the dock tractors would be coupled by means of longish coupling chains. Without buffers, any sudden stop would result in the timber coming together between adjacent bogies. The wagons are internal user, stencilled "Dock Use Only", after being declared unfit for main line work. They finished their lives in useful service here, where they could stand loaded for considerable periods after arrival of a timber ship. It is believed that during LNER days the 'dock only' wagons were painted all over green. By the BR period this was reduced to a green panel for the numbers only. Such was the state of some of that it was not unknown during a rough shunt for a wagon to break up or pull a drawhook out of the headstock.

An interesting mid–1960s view taken from Southcoates Lane road bridge, looking west. Although two world wars and 50 years have intervened the layout is much as the NER left it in the summer of 1914. Southcoates Lane signal box had, until its eventual destruction by enemy action, been on the extreme right. Centre is the purpose–built 1914 connection to the H&BR; this joined the parent system at Bridge Junction (Newbridge Road), 952 yards away. Originally laid as a double line and long out of use, by the time of this picture it had been reduced to single line, and there is obviously some P.W. work in evidence. Over on the right are the Up and Down Withernsea lines, these being diverted onto this formation in 1914 with the opening of the new Joint Dock. Behind are the usual lineside allotments, and further to the north the houses of Belmont Street. On the south, or left, side can be seen the goods lines and sidings, providing a through route between Southcoates station and Holderness Drain North signalboxes, connecting the King George Dock with the low level Victoria Dock branch. Originally the double slip and much of the pointwork, including the now long–removed signalling, had been worked from the signal box. Photograph Ian K. Watson.

Southcoates Lane signal box was built by the NER to work their end of the new connection to the H&BR. This was opened about 1914 to allow trains to pass to and from either company's lines and also to work onto the new King George Dock. Within days of its opening the Great War started, the railways came under government control and the need to transfer trains between the two systems more or less ceased. Eventually the signal box was temporarily closed, and appears to have been out of use until as late as March 1924. With the severe trade depressions of the 1920s and 1930s the connection to the H&B section was again taken out of use and Southcoates would have once more been temporarily closed. Of course with both sections under the common ownership of the LNER the original reason to transfer traffic had long ceased. In all probability Southcoates Lane would have closed officially in November 1938, the date when its H&BR counterpart Bridges Junction was last in use. The picture dates from 13th July 1943 and shows the damage done to both the signal box and nearby bridge by a Luftwaffe bombing raid. The lines directly in front of the signal box are those of the Withernsea branch; actually this is the rear wall of the structure and although much damaged by the blast, it is obvious that the lever frame and all inside fittings had been removed long before. For some reason the signal box was built wider than usual, at one end only, and this resulted in an L–shaped building. The remains of the box were demolished almost immediately, before work commenced on removing the blown–out bridge spans. Until this was done the Withernsea branch was effectively closed. The spire in the left background belongs to Hedon Road gaol; some thirty years later it was to become notorious when prison riots became popular.

(opposite top) This picture was captured on the same day and clearly shows the wholesale devastation meted out by the enemy bombers. The main target was undoubtedly the nearby docks, Alexandra dock being a mere stones' throw to the left. Under the felled bridge span is the junction and the beginning of the climb to the HB Section. This had been out of use for quite some years but was reinstated as from Tuesday 24th February 1942, to form an emergency diversion route in case of enemy action. Unfortunately it is not known if it was ever used for that purpose. A ground frame was provided to work the junction and the new signals. Of interest here, is the direction signal, an NER lower quadrant, and obviously recovered from elsewhere. This must have been one of the very last occasions when a 'new' LQ signal was put into service. Despite the apparent mess and damage the permanent way was soon relaid and brought back into use. The signal showing 'clear' is not a result of the bomb damage – the route was permanently laid towards Southcoates station and the Victoria dock branch. Therefore the top arm or left hand route was always at clear for normal through running. The distant signal is on the Withernsea branch, and belongs to Southcoates signal box. The branch lines are not visible here, being hidden behind the long grass. This view also illustrates well the additional width of the east end of the Southcoates Lane signal box. When first brought into use there was the usual complement of signals in typical NER tradition. A large iron signal bridge had spanned the lines to the foreground of this view but unfortunately no photographs are known to survive; this and the previous picture are believed to be the only remaining record of the box.

(opposite bottom) Following the air raid of 14th July 1943, and its total destruction, Southcoates Lane road bridge was eventually rebuilt. Possibly owing to the wartime shortages of both labour and materials, it appears to have been a protracted job. Eighteen months later and with the war almost won, the new span by December 1944 was nearly ready for the laying in of the roadway.

57

90009 at Marfleet with the Hedon Pickup on the morning of 30th March 1966. The road bridge in the background was a 1930s replacement for a level crossing. Although the station had been closed to passengers for 18 months the name board was still intact. The J16 Pilot left shed at 5.15 am and ran to Inward Yard for 'Goods Empties', it then tripped to Drypool returning afterwards to Inward Yard. A further trip was made to Drypool and Wilmington, running as 'engine and van'. At Drypool an additional brake van was attached, simplifying the working of Messrs. Wade's groundframe (between Marfleet and Hedon). J16 is seen here en route to Hedon, on what was then the remains of the Withernsea branch. On return it will shunt Wade's Siding, Marfleet, Drypool, Wilmington, and Stepney, and then onto Empty Mineral yard. Goods facilities at Marfleet consisted a single siding with a total standage length of 151 yards. Originally there had been two main to main crossovers, one at each end of the station, but eventually the one at the west end was taken out, a fate shared with many other NER stations. Marfleet signal box was brought into use during late 1903 and replaced what had previously been described in official records as a 'signal box wood cover on platform'. This original 'signal box' had contained a frame of seven levers. The new works and double line of railway were inspected by the Board of Trade on 11th December 1903 – at this time, of the 25 levers provided, 19 were in use. After a life of almost 65 years Marfleet box closed on 28th October 1968.

Marfleet looking towards the east. This is an undated picture, but judging by the state of the track is taken after 3rd June 1968 when the line to Hedon was abandoned. Alongside the Up platform is a 350 hp diesel shunter hauling a ballast train which appears to consist of recovered track panels. Stories abound of a one–time station master here who was, by all accounts, as mad as a hatter and sat with a cardboard box over his head. A successor had the appropriate surname of Train – he was in office when one the authors arrived at Marfleet station in July 1931 to begin a 41 year stint of work in Hull.

ANLABY ROAD TO HESSLE ROAD & TO COTTINGHAM SOUTH

An evocative 1958 Saturday afternoon view of what the local train spotters called the 'Shed Crocodile'. These four engines have worked all the week out-stationed at Dry-pool and are waiting at Anlaby Road Junction for a suitable path back to Dairycoates shed. Lashed prominently to three of the engines are the crews' push bikes often, in those days, their sole means of transport. Only the locomotive nearest the camera can be identified as J72 No.68746. Above the leading engine can be seen Anlaby Road Up goods home signal with the outer distant of St Georges Road Gate box below. This will have been erected circa 1904 as a typical NER lower quadrant slotted post signal. Of interest – only the top arm has been renewed, as an upper quadrant, and the post has lost its characteristic McKenzie & Holland finial. These alterations were made July 20th, 1952.

Looking west from the 'six foot' of the main lines towards Anlaby Road Junction and level crossing. The signal on the right is the Up Victoria Dock branch Home, with St Georges Road Distant below. The railwayman's cottage was demolished to make way for the Cottingham branch.

With the opening of the Paragon station almost two miles of new railway and several level crossings were brought into use. The largest and most important of these was at Anlaby Road, seen here on 14th March 1955, looking towards Hessle Road. Anlaby Road became a junction when the Victoria Dock branch was first opened for goods traffic on 16th May 1853. Passenger trains commenced almost three weeks later on 1st June, and for some time after passengers for the branch were set down or picked up on the level crossing. Proper platforms were never provided, and eventually the practice was to cease. In this view the junction points are behind the camera, and therefore unseen. Beyond the footbridge is the picturesque splay cornered signal box, this was probably built sometime in 1875 as part of the NER's on-going policy to introduce the 'Block' system. The signal box remained in use for a further 89 years and just managed to outlive the level crossing. Like at Hessle Road almost two years before, there was something of a civic ceremony. The Lord Mayor first drove over the new flyover, and then went up to the signal box, and himself closed the gates for the last time, at approx 7 p.m. on Friday 31st July 1964.

Anlaby Road crossing 9th June 1961 with B1 No.61215 WILLIAM HENTON CARVER bringing in a Kings Cross train from Doncaster. The signals are off for the main line to West Parade junction and Paragon, whilst the others are for the Victoria Dock branch. Photograph Peter Rose.

Looking west through Anlaby Road gates during the early months of 1955. Practically all of this scene was swept away during the mid–1960s with the building of the flyover. Apart from the buildings in the middle background little remains today, though fortunately for modern mums Persil still washes whiter.

On a warm summer's day in 1959 Class J73 No.68360, of Dairycoates shed, steams 'light engine' past Hessle Road signalbox, no doubt bound for the Permanent Way yard just north of the level crossing. According to the official publication 'Authorised Pilot and Shunting engines Hull District' of April 1957, No.22A pilot was 'engaged from 8.00 a.m. to midnight SX and from 6.00 a.m. to 9 p.m. SO, to Shunt Storeyard, Trips Storeyard to Inward Yard, assist with Fish traffic and deal with fish empties'.

Heading west for Doncaster Class D49/2 No.62763 THE FITZWILLIAM storms past Hessle Road signal box with the four car Hull portion of the Yorkshire Pullman.

Framed by the railwaymen's houses on one side and the crossing keepers cottages on the other, Class V1 No.67640 heads for Paragon sometime in 1959. In all probability the train, which is loaded to at least seven bogies, will be an early evening Brough workmans' return train. These trains, run to cater for the employees of the Blackburn aircraft factory, were for many years a regular feature of local train working. *Sans* smokebox shed plate No.67640 was one of the last steam locos to be transferred to Botanic Gardens shed, arriving in September 1958. Even so this was to be a short lived move for only ten months later, along with all its stable mates, 67640 was reallocated the following June to Dairycoates. The typical chalked front buffer instructions readily suggest this picture was taken after the shed transfer. On the right is the long siding leading to the Permanent Way Dept. yard, referred to locally simply as 'Store yard'.

The doom and gloom that was the old Hessle Road. In this view, looking west, the scene is wholly dominated by the railway. Overhead and carried across the roadway by bridge No.8 is the Neptune Street branch of the H&BR. At ground level are the lines of the main Hull to Selby route. They had their origin in the Hull & Bridlington branch of the Hull & Selby Railway and were brought into use on November 2nd 1846. From the earliest days a signalbox has existed here, and as long ago as December 1867, reporting on an accident between the 10.10 a.m. Hull – Speeton goods, and the 10.40 a.m. Hull – Leeds passenger train, Captain Tyler of the Board of Trade remarked:- *This junction has been provided with a good cabin, containing levers for working the main signals, the distant signals, and the points; supplied with Saxby and Farmers locking apparatus; and provided with a wheel by which the signalman can work the gates of the level crossing simultaneously without leaving his post. The line is level in all directions, but is only visible, in consequence of a curve and some buildings, for a short distance towards the Hull passenger station. The main signals are all of them over the junction stage, and the distant signals toward the Hull passenger station and the Hull goods station are respectively about 600 and 400 yards from that stage. Between the stage and the latter distant signal there are some sidings.* In the above view, taken on 17th March 1953, peeping out from under the footbridge can be seen the bay window protrusion of the signal box. This was probably added to the existing structure during 1914, in readiness for working the electric trams across the railway. A feature of the Hull level crossings was the provision of special tram signals and catch points. These were worked by the railway signalman and in addition to the gates provided extra protect on to the railway. Across the road on the bridge abutment can be seen the sign proclaiming 'BR Dairycoates Depot'. This refers to the coal

high level embankment and the NER P.W. depot. Long before the great influx of the private car and the road haulage industry Hull's numerous level crossings were a curse. Hessle Road was the most notorious and an LNER document of 1927 provided the statistics that between the hours of 6.00 a.m. and 11.00 p.m. daily, the gates were shut for a total period of 6 hours and 52 minutes, or 138 times! At about the same time the LNER drew up an elaborate plan to eliminate all of the city's level crossings. These were to be presented to the 1929/30 session of parliament, but probably as a result of the 1930s trade depression were never heard of again. A similar plan was again mooted in the early post-war years, but this again came to nothing. Ten years later a definite scheme to eliminate the level crossing problem was proposed and Hessle Road was the first to be eliminated. Work was well under way by late 1961 or early 1962, but before this could be completed, on the west side of the railway all trains were diverted from the high level H&BR branch. All traffic from the Neptune Street branch was now brought down to ground level from a new embankment. Via a new junction this was connected to the existing low level railway, and was brought into partial use from 5th March 1962. Three weeks later, on Sunday 25th March, bridge No.8 was removed – work now progressed at a rapid rate, and by the summer contractors were completing the main span. Such was the progress that on Saturday 15th September and accompanied with much civic acclaim, at 6.15 p.m. the Lord Mayor was driven over the completed half of the flyover. His car returned through the level crossing which then remained permanently closed to road traffic. The mechanical signal box remained in use for a further three weeks and was officially closed at 12.01 a.m. on Sun 7th October 1962, when at the same time the present box with its 'NX' push button panel was commissioned.

Hessle Road looking east from under the H&BR towards the town centre. The wooden hut on the left was, until made redundant by the road traffic lights, the domain of the gate man. It was his duty to walk out with a red flag and stop the road traffic, to assist the signalman.

When no longer required by the Traffic Department, the hut with its roaring coal fire became a convenient winter retreat for the linemen and signal fitters of the S & T Department. The stark building behind was for many years the Railway Institute.

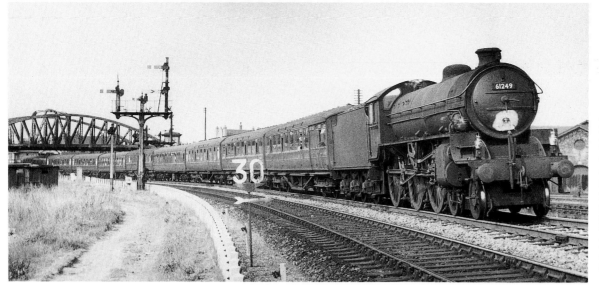

Sheffield Darnall B1 No.61249 FITZHER-BERT WRIGHT attacks the steep gradient which will eventually carry the main Hull to Selby railway over the mineral lines at Dairy-coates. The train, with its mixture of Gresley, Thompson, and BR MK1 stock is almost certainly an afternoon departure to Sheffield.

Ex LNER 'Green Arrow' No.60812 passes mile post 2 sometime during 1959 with an Up express passenger train for Leeds.

Ex–Ministry of Supply 0–6–0ST No.68042 of LNER class J94 working bunker first with a train of sawn timber. The trip, No.133 and the class J headlamp suggest the train has originated from the many rail connected sawmills in the Drypool area. It will have worked across from the east of the city via the Victoria Dock branch and joined the main line at Anlaby Road junction. Here the train is just one mile further on, now leaving the main line, and heading towards Dairy-coates West signal box and its eventual des-tination, Outward Yard.

With only a few months of useful life left Class D49/1 No.62707 LANCASHIRE heads an unidentified Up express over Hessle Road junction. Above is the bow string girder bridge carrying the former H&BR Neptune Street branch. This bridge, which had a life of almost 77 years, was made redundant on March 5th 1962, when that branch, in connection with the stage work for the new flyover, was diverted. In all, the removal of the bridge and its abutments was spread over a period of four weeks. Initially between the 5th–10th March the P.W. Department were engaged to remove the track, whilst during this same week contractors took out the bridge decking. On Sunday 11th March in readiness to remove the main spans the 'X' bracing girders between them were cut away. The following Sunday saw great activity when the York, Hull and Darlington steam cranes were employed to remove one of the main spans. A week later, on Sunday 25th March, and again using the same technique, the remaining span was removed. Both weekends involved a total blockage of the passenger lines from 1.00 a.m. Sunday for 24 hours, and during this period all trains commenced or terminated at Hessle. With this work complete the contractors were allocated a further week until 31st March to demolish the remains of the brick abutments. Nevertheless, even today a short portion of the old embankment remains, opposite the present Hessle Road signal box.

After the passage of the Fridays–only 3.13 pm Brough – Hull (to the right, to Paragon), J14 pilot 90670 comes off the H&BR high level line on 5th July 1963 with a train from King George Dock, which includes four wagons of molasses for BOCM at Selby. Beyond the rear of the train is the Chalk Lane permanent way storeyard, where an 0–4–0 diesel, Departmental No.56, operated. Next right is the line to Cottingham South, part of the original Hull – Bridlington line. To the right of this is Chalk Lane coal yard with, on this day, only one wagon present. A housing estate now occupies the site of the PW store yard, Newington branch and Chalk Lane coal sidings.

Hessle Road looking east to the town centre. Construction of the new flyover was already underway when this view was taken on 27th October 1961. Although there are road traffic lights the gates remained (unlike Walton Street) mechanically worked. The engine is 61189 SIR WILLIAM GREY running light to Paragon to work the 1.07 pm parcels to Scarborough. By this date steam working on the Scarborough line was becoming pretty thin on the ground. In readiness for laying in the new North branch the old houses, which once occupied the foreground, have been demolished. Similarly, across the road the pedestrian footbridge is now removed. The houses were in Trinidad Street. The Limmer & Trinidad Lake Asphalte Co. had opened works in what was known as Ash Street and a variety of other names: in 1925 their application for this new name to avoid confusion was agreed.

Snaking round the seemingly unnecessary S bend Class B1 No.61306, working local pilot trip J19 on 29th July 1963, threads its train of empty mineral wagons through Hessle Road Junction. The train has worked down from the high level, former H&BR, and is here joining the new North branch connections. These new goods lines came into partial use on 5th March 1962. The rest of the colour light signalling, the altered connections from the high level H&B lines and the new signal box opened at 12.1 a.m. Sunday 7th October 1962. In the left middle background, remnants of the original H&BR embankment are visible; it was almost 25 years later before these were finally removed. The main Hull to Selby lines are to the right of the picture, and, just visible, the junction with the Bridlington branch. 61087 drifts by with a Bridlington train routed along the Newington branch to Cottingham South, where it will join the line from Paragon. photograph Peter Rose.

The camera has caught a splendid mix of both the new and old order at Hessle Road on 16th January 1962. Within weeks the H&BR Neptune Street branch will be swept away, and trains diverted onto new goods lines which have yet to be laid directly in front of the new signal box. Overhead a Class B1 (probably 61289) is working a local trip of oil tanks from the Saltend refinery. Its destination is Albert Dock signal box about a mile further east – here the engine will run round and by means of the 'exchange sidings', transfer the train onto the former NER metals. Disappearing in the distance on the Down main, complete with the 'cats whisker' version of the present day yellow warning panel, is a Paragon bound DMU bearing the reporting number 2H63. Later Class 110, the Birmingham RC&W dmu was then commonly known as a Calder Valley Unit, working that route across the Pennines to Manchester. The signal was originally a three doll bracket, but was altered in October 1952 to incorporate a fourth doll. From left to right the signals are No.23 Up Dairycoates branch to PW Yard; No.24 Up Dairycoates branch to Down Cottingham branch; No.63 Up Dairycoates branch to Goods Yard; No.25 Up Dairycoates Branch to Down Main with Chalk Lane Outer Distant below.

Hessle Road looking south, Friday 5th July 1963. This view shows off both the new North branch and signal box to advantage. At the time of its opening the provision of central heating, inside toilet, and a separate kitchen was something of an innovation. If nothing else the signalman at the end of each shift no longer had to lug buckets of coal and ash up and down the stairs.

1C92, the return working of 1H92, the summer Saturday Bradford – Bridlington train, approaching Hessle Road junction on the line from Cottingham South with Jubilee 45694 BELLEROPHON at the head. The date is 25th July 1964. Low Moor shed was responsible for this working but when that shed was short of power a variety of engines from other depots would be used. Photograph Peter Rose.

From Hessle Road junction to Cottingham South the goods–only line ran virtually due north crossing two main roads on its way to the latter place. The first of these was Anlaby Road at Newington and in this 1964 view we see the former signal box of 1899 vintage just a year before closure. By now Newington box had been down graded to a non–block post and housed only the apparatus for controlling the level crossing gates. The passenger train used to gain this photograph was in fact a 'special' organised to visit the goods–only and dock lines around Hull. Photograph Ian.K.Watson.

Waterworks crossing 20th April 1963. Many years ago a short siding had existed here, and a tramway led off it from a wagon turntable to serve the Springhead waterworks. This same siding was also used during the construction of the Hull & Barnsley Railway, as a railhead for the delivery of building materials. With the completion of the new railway in July 1885 the Hull Corporation, as might be expected, nailed its colours to the H&BR mast. The tramway was connected to both railways for some time afterwards but was eventually truncated, and all links with the NER were severed. It is known to have still been in existence during 1890 but is not mentioned in a Board of Trade inspection report of August 1899. This related to the Hessle Road, Cottingham Junction branch being converted to double track, and also to a temporary signal box. The latter was little more than a wooden hut containing only nine levers, of which seven were in use. It stood on the down side of the line just south of the H&BR bridge, and was specially erected to work the northern end of the showground sidings, brought into use that year. There is no mention of a level crossing existing at this date, and according to the records of the NER, the signal box was dispensed with on 21st March 1906. Following the Great War, and to cope with the ever increasing need for housing, the city gradually expanded to the west. Springbank West was extended westward and a new level crossing provided over the Newington branch. The cost of the new works was met by the Hull Corporation, an LNER minute of 2nd October 1924 declaring: 'Provision of gates and signals at the Springbank level crossing. Contract to the Westinghouse Brake & Saxby Signal Co. £1021 18/ 9d, this amount to be paid by the Hull Corporation'. Four days later, on 6th October, the equipment was ordered, and the contract with the Westinghouse Co. formally agreed. Amongst this was a 20 lever locking frame of the usual No.16 pattern, works No.9499. It was originally intended to extend the existing Springbank tram route of the Hull Corporation to the west, over both Walton Street and the new Waterworks level crossings, but through the opposition of the LNER this came to nothing. By the time of its actual installation the interlocking frame only contained seven levers and two gate wheels. It is probable that the planned extra capacity of the lever frame had been intended for the tram signals and catch points. Whatever, the signal box and level crossing were brought into use some time during the early months of 1925; all of the equipment, though supplied two years after the North Eastern had ceased to exist, was to the familiar pattern long used by that company. Similarly, the all–brick signal box was to the NER S4 pattern, and as fate would later dictate it was the final example of this type to be built new in the city. In fact as the photograph well illustrates the whole set–up was very reminiscent of the pre–war Hornby set. Forty years on, on May 23rd 1965, the Newington branch was abandoned and the signal box and level crossing fell out of use. Photograph I.K. Watson.

Just two miles out from Hull Paragon, and with the works of Messrs. Ideal Standard Ltd. as a backdrop, class V1 2–6–2T No.67640, with a short stopping passenger train, negotiates Cottingham South Junction. The lines to the right are those of the original Hull and Bridlington branch of 1846, which lost all regular passenger traffic in 1848, when Paragon station opened, replacing Manor House station of 1840. This short 1¾ mile branch between Hessle Road Junction and Cottingham South Junction remained single line for many years, and it was as late as 1899 before it eventually became double track. Known as 'Straight Line' by the local train spotters the branch, which permitted through excursion trains direct access to the Bridlington branch without reversing at Paragon, remained in use until May 23rd 1965. Photograph N. Stead.

H&BR FROM DAIRYCOATES TO KING GEORGE DOCK

During its construction the H&BR was measured from the Cudworth or western end, but upon completion the whole line was remeasured from the buffer stops at Alexandra Dock emigrant passenger station. In April 1924, using a new datum point approximately twelve chains west of Alexandra Dock Junction, the LNER again remeasured the railway. After this latest exercise new mileposts of ex–NER pattern were provided. Left is the new 'Zero post' erected on the Alexandra Dock; whilst the letters H(AD) are self evident the letter S is worth a brief mention. Although called the Hull & Barnsley the railway never reached the later town, and in fact terminated at Stairfoot. Right is milepost 3 which was a short distance to the east of the Ella Street sidings. Both the above have been purchased through the official channels, and are now in private collections.

One of the closest cities to Germany, Hull and its railways were a prime target for enemy action. Following such an incident a former H&BR 0–6–2T of Class N13, No.2534, is seen in a precarious position on 22nd February 1941 on the ex–H&BR Neptune Street branch near to Haltemprice Street; the houses to the left are those in North Road. 2534 seems to have been little damaged, and was put back into traffic, to be eventually withdrawn from Neville Hill shed as No.69116 in December 1954. This picture is looking almost due north, and the H&BR Dairy-coates Yard can be seen down at ground level on the right.

Boothferry Park halt 21st June 1963 with B1 No.61012 PUKU heading north with a short train on J21 Pilot. Photograph Peter Rose.

BR Standard 77002 is loaded with 12 empty minerals and a brake van whilst working trip J04 past the single platform Boothferry Park halt. The train is bound for Empty Mineral yard having previously shunted the coal depots at Ella St. and Sculcoates. The single line is the connection to the H&BR Dairycoates coal depot, and is 60 chains in length, raising on a gradient of 1 in 120. Although the depot was shown on a map as long ago as 1890, it was 1st May 1905 before it was actually brought into use. The single line was worked 'No Block' as a long siding. Originally access was via a trailing slip connection worked from Springbank South signal box. On Wednesday 3rd September 1930 a facing connection was brought into use to enable direct access for contractors trains. These were working from Kirkella Cutting with chalk, in–fill for the new Inward Yard then under construction. At the same time a through connection was made from the Dairycoates Sidings (HB) to the NE system. This was left in after the completion of the Inward Yard and was later used for some engine and van and pilot workings. In an emergency trains could also be diverted by this route. *"...Wednesday 3 September 1930. Springbank South – New facing Connection No.12 Points, brought into use this day. By use of clamps, for contractors trains running between Kirkella Cutting and New Inward Yard. Marker boards with telephone erected in order that trains proceeding from Hessle Road box, or from Dairycoates H&B or Coal depot (H&B) may telephone Springbank South signalman for permission to proceed up the single line to No.13 signal Springbank South".* Previously only one train was allowed in Dairycoates H&B to shunt the sidings and coal depot; when ready to propel his train up the single line to No.13 signal the driver whistled one crow intimating, to the signalman that he required to pass from Dairycoates Siding onto the Up Main. After passing through No.11 points and slip, he was ready to proceed with his load to Neptune Street H&B. After 3rd September 1930 pilots in and out of Dairycoates H&B sidings used this marker board during the period contractors trains were running. The connections at the Hessle Road end onto the NER Section was left and later used for engines and vans, and for some pilots running off Dock Branch to Dairycoates. The connections at Springbank South were taken out of use as from 23rd April 1967. Dairycoates single line was known locally as 'the snicket'. Photograph Peter Rose.

Shipment coal formed a large proportion of the traffic over the H&BR high level line. 90427, JO1 pilot has 'a breath of steam on', passing Springbank South with a load of empty mineral wagons from Alexandra Dock on 21st June 1963. Springbank South signal box worked the southern tip of the Springhead triangular junction, usually referred to as 'the Angle'. In earlier days when Springhead turntable was out of use the angle was also used for turning engines. At the time of this picture, the late signalman Alan Moor was in charge of South box. His glistening windows, and general cleanliness would have been the pride of many a housewife. After being on 'shift only' to serve Springhead, the box eventually closed on 4th May 1968, when the area of Hessle Road panel was extended. The line to Springhead bears off to the left behind the engine. Springbank South, though surrounded by houses, never had running water and remained oil lit throughout its 83 year life. Officially the water was brought in cans from Springhead by one of the pilots, but in later years at least it became the practice to scrounge water from any nearby friendly housewife. As from 29th November 1958, with the abandonment of the H&B as a through line and the closing of Springhead shed, both Springbank South and West boxes had their hours reduced. These were now 8.50 a.m. – 4.10 p.m. six days per week; there were no rest days, and the hours just balanced exactly the 44 hour week worked by railwaymen. Useful overtime could be made at both boxes, usually during the week when Hull City were playing an evening match. Springbank South had to be open to cross the football trains facing road into the single platform, while in the more heady days of the 1960s the empty stock and engines were often stored at Springhead. To put things in perspective, in 1962 the West signalman (being Class 2) would be on £10 11s 0d per week, whilst his unfortunate colleague at South box, being only Class 4, would receive the princely sum of £10 4s 0d for his labours. Ironically, by the nature of such things it was the South box that did all the hard graft. Photograph Peter Rose.

Looking west on September 18th 1964 from the windows of Springbank North box. 'Control orders' pilot JO5 with Austerity 2–8–0 No.90478, of Dairycoates shed, heads its load of export motor cars towards King George Dock on the Down Main from Springbank South. The brakevan is just clear of the junction at Springbank South, indicating the train is about a quarter mile in length. The signal is a standard BR 'plate and angle bracket' and in March 1957 had replaced the original H&BR example. By this time the signalling had become an interesting mix of HBR, NER lower quadrants and two BR upper quadrants. These were the Up Main Starting signals, and were: left hand doll to Springbank South, middle to Springhead via Springbank West. The right hand empty doll had until 29th June 1964 signalled trains towards Loco Junction via the now long–disused main line. Close inspection in the 'six foot' below reveals the now redundant and bent arm laying forgotten, cast aside by the signal fitter almost 30 summers ago. Down below at ground level, running from north to south, the afternoon sun reflects off the metals of the Hessle Road to Cottingham South (Newington) branch. To the right is Jacksons' builders yard – the younger of the two authors, along with his many school pals, used it as a playground, excavating out the brick stacks and building the mandatory 'den'. The signal bracket seen in this picture was taken down in March 1968, and re–erected for further use in the Normanton area. Photograph Peter Rose.

90008 passes Springbank North box, ex–H&BR on a dull 18th April 1963. Beyond the roadbridge, a curve goes down to join the ex–NER at Walton Street Jct. This was laid in July 1924 to enable H&BR passenger trains to use Paragon instead of Cannon St. The picture is taken from the Up Main Starter bracket signal, looking east, in the down direction. This is the replacement signal box built by the LNER to work the existing junctions and the new connections to the NER Scarborough branch. Although built 18 months into the LNER period, the box is a standard NER design; being on an embankment it is of all–wood construction, on wooden piles. Photograph Peter Rose.

On July 13th 1924 the Cannon Street terminus of the former H&BR was reduced to goods only, and from the following day all passenger services diverted to Paragon. The two systems were linked by a new railway constructed on an embankment to the north side of Spring Bank West. This commenced just beyond Walton Street level crossing, and joined the H&BR east of the overhead railway bridge. When this picture was taken on 7th April 1955 the Hull to South Howden passenger service was doomed, to be withdrawn some four months later, on 1st August. The engine is G5 No.67280 running bunker first with the four coaches of the 7.53 a.m. South Howden to Hull. Behind the engine is the one–time H&BR main line to Cannon Street and Alexandra Dock, now goods only. The signal on the right is Springbank North up goods home, lever No.41. A typical NER slotted post signal, it was first brought into use on Sunday 29th June 1924, to protect the new junction. Similarly the two doll balanced bracket seen in the background Down Main Starting (3) with Walton St distant (4) below and Down Main to Down Goods Starting (4) was also brought into use on the same day. The Up Main home signal (44) has already succumbed to progress and has been replaced by a standard British Railways tubular post upper quadrant signal. This remained in use until Saturday May 4th 1968; when the signal box closed, whilst both the remaining lower quadrant signals had been replaced during the early months of 1957. Railway modellers might care to note the rough appearance of both the track and ballast. Photograph N.E. Stead.

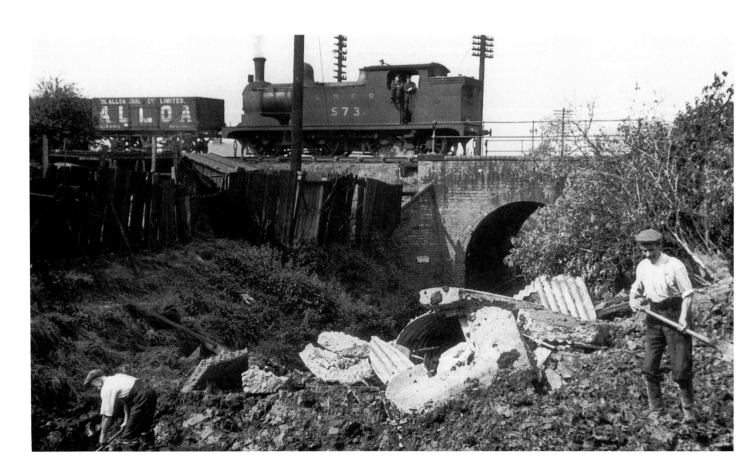

Newland Avenue bridge circa 1962. While the NER made the city into one of level crossings the H&BR made it into one of numerous bridges. In all the Hull and Barnsley provided Hull with somewhere in the region of 45 bridges, though not all of them, admittedly, over the public highway. Typical of the smaller spans is Bridge No.27; not quite three miles to the west of Alexandra Dock, this was part of the original railway of 1885, and is still in use today. No.1 had been an impressive girder bridge spanning Hedon Road immediately north of the Alexandra Dock. When the rail connection to Alexandra Dock was taken out of use on Monday 24th January 1983, No.1 fell into disuse, and was eventually demolished in the late 1980s. Unaware of the camera the original 'Angry Young Man', complete with duffle coat, cycles past – dating this view to the early 'sixties and the dawn of the Beatnik era. Thirty years on we are still wondering what promise Mackeson has to offer, but (unlike the ales of Moors & Robson's advertised above) at least it is still with us. The trolley bus fleet No.67 was the first of a batch of twelve identical vehicles supplied to Hull Corporation new in 1945. These had Sunbeam W chassis fitted with Metropolitan–Vickers electrical equipment, and a Brush 7′ 6″ wide H30/26R body. All were withdrawn for scrap during 1962–63. The Newland Avenue No.62 trolley bus service commenced on 3rd October 1937, and ceased on 16 November 1963.

(opposite) Ella Street 2nd September 1941, looking north at the H&BR Ella Street sidings. On the drain bank two workmen clean off the damage from a previous air raid. This is without doubt a specially posed picture; under normal working no fireman would have the time to sit like that on the cab side sheet. The train is stood on the Down main, and in all probability will eventually draw forward, and then set back to shunt the Ella Street coal yard. Next to the engine is a typical Scottish private owner wagon, once the property of the ALLOA coal company, but now as part of the war effort 'pooled' under government control. The bridge spans the Cottingham drain, which is now filled in, and today forms a convenient walkway. Ella Street signal box (of which no photographs are known to exist) stood on the extreme left until it was abolished in 1937. The locomotive is of former NER Class B, later Class N8, built as long ago as December 1889, and eventually ended its days in May 1955 as 69392.

The Hull & Barnsley's Beverley Road station was actually in Fitzroy Street, and was the first station on the main line proper. Being easily accessible from the town centre originally by the horse, and from 1900 by the electric trams, it was often more popular as an embarking point than the main terminus at Cannon Street. When the passenger service was diverted to Paragon station on July 14th 1924 it was closed entirely. The Up & Down platforms were eventually taken away, and the remains of the building became almost completely divorced from the railway. After less than forty years of railway service the buildings were either let off or sold, and for a time were used by an engineering company. Access between the two platforms had been via a subway through the embankment, used at one time during the last war as a communal air raid shelter. Unlike its near neighbour at Cannon Street, Beverley Road survived just long enough to see the H&BR centenary in 1985. The end finally came in 1986, when what was then little more than a derelict and windowless slum finally succumbed to the demolition men.

One of those 'last train' pictures of Cannon Street terminus. This is 2429 clearing empty stock on the day after the last passenger train had left.

A Gas works was first established at the Bankside site by the British Gas Light Company Ltd. in 1824. The site grew to over 41 acres, attaining a maximum production capacity of 60 million cubic feet of gas per day. The advent of natural gas from the North Sea brought about closure in 1973 after 149 years of continuous production. A network of tracks ran around the site which was serviced by the company's own shunting locomotives. Overbridges across Bankside itself were also constructed, to serve hoppers for the loading of coke and other by-products onto shipping moored at the wharf on the River Hull. The gas works was not rail connected until the coming of the H&BR in July 1885, to the north of and across the line from the Sculcoates Goods yard. In this 1924 picture the gas works, holder and private sidings predominate, whilst just visible on the extreme left are the sidings of the H&BR goods yard. Forty years later these same sidings would become the final resting place for several hundred steam locomotives. The wooden clad cooling towers belong to the Hull Corporation Sculcoates Electricity Department. Photo reproduced by kind permission of Mal Baker.

K1s were never allocated to any Hull sheds but from time to time did work into the city and on more than one occasion were borrowed to work a local pilot trip. Of the 732 engines cut up by Drapers 17 were K1s. 62012, a one time West Highland engine, is seen in Drapers yard on 29th August 1967, the day after its cutting up had commenced. Behind are sister engines 62001 and 62065. To the left is the cooling tower of Sculcoates power station – it too was to be made redundant. The tower being demolished by explosions at 7.20 am on 31st October 1979, after which all the errant TV repair men and aerial erectors in the North Hull area had to find a new excuse for their faulty workmanship. Photograph Peter Rose.

Apart from the Alexandra Dock which is no longer railway owned the only major surviving works of the H&BR are the embankments which circumvent the city, intersecting almost every major road and not a few side streets. The river Hull is crossed by means of a high level swing bridge not far upstream from the NER Sculcoates bridge. During the early months of 1988 most of this surviving remnant of the H&BR was reduced to single track. Seen here from the cab of a diesel locomotive is the former Down line traversing the girders of the river bridge. The signal box originates from H&BR times, and was opened with the line in July 1885. This ceased to be a 'Block Post' over 60 years ago, and ever since has only been manned as required, usually at high water. At some time the signal box, which originally had a hipped roof, was extensively rebuilt. Further evidence of this are the metal framed windows, and the difference in both the colour and bonding of the brick work. Inside, some of the original Saxby & Farmer levers remain in use, whilst outside the bridge is little altered. Photograph Steve Bramley.

The Hull & Barnsley Railway had established a two road, timber built, engine shed at Alexandra Dock. By 1913 this was in such a ramshackle state that it was beyond repair, and was in need of replacement. In reality it remained in use until December 1927, but was then demolished, no new shed being provided, and thereafter engines stood out in the open. This is an undated view from the 1950s, a number of diesel shunters have already ousted some of the steam locos from their duties. The diesels are stabled on what was once one of the shed roads. The pilot numbers are not known.

Class J71 No.286 was already 50 years old when this view was first exposed during the September of 1938. Despite its advancing years a further two decades were to elapse before this venerable engine, as BR No.68242, was finally withdrawn in August 1958. The crude wire basket spark arrester stands up clumsily and prominently from the chimney. On an engine employed almost exclusively to shunt the docks and nearby timber yards this was a most useful and necessary device. On the left is one of the many, typical, examples of stacked timber – in this case pit props. These will eventually be used in the pits of the South Yorkshire coalfields, making the journey in what would otherwise be the returning empty coal wagons. The signal box in the background is Holderness Drain South, the H&BR contribution to the signalling on King George Dock. With a 50 lever interlocking frame it was brought into use during the summer of 1914. Surprisingly, despite the gross rationalisations of the 1960s, the signal box and a couple of sidings lingered on until December 1973.

From the mid–1890s the H&BR used the contractors Evans O'Donnel for all their signalling equipment. A typical example is seen here near the Alexandra Dock, though it was actually worked from Holderness Drain South box. This is the Up Home signal from the jetties or 'NE Corner', lever No.42, 14th June 1961. By the time this example was brought into use for the opening of King George Dock in 1914 Messrs. Evans had become part of Saxby & Farmer. It was one of the last lower quadrant signals to remain in use in the city and it is now over 25 years since the last example of an HB signal was taken out of use – nevertheless, near–identical ones remain in South America.

Owing to the lack of any turning facilities tender first running on the local pilot trips was common. Here 90262 is seen with the J10 pilot, passing Alexandra Dock signal box en route to Saltend. With its 80–odd levers, Alexandra Dock signal box had been the largest on the H&BR. Built in 1910 it replaced the original of 1885 and survived until May 1974. Messrs. Sangwins, a local building firm, were responsible for its erection at a contract price of £310 19s 11d. The signalling work and new locking frame was contracted out on 25th May 1909 to Saxby & Farmer at a total cost of £1,150. By 1958 the lever frame was worn out and replaced by one of 90 made up in York locking shop from recovered material. The writing was already on the wall for mechanical signalling and as it happened this was one of the last big frames to be built there. At the same time the outside signalling was modified and brought up to date and by 20th January 1967, the date of this picture, all the signals were replaced by BR types. Within five months steam working from Dairycoates shed had come to an end, and for the final weeks of its life 90272 was transferred to Goole. It was withdrawn from there in June of 1967, and then once more returned to Hull to meet its destiny at Drapers scrap yard, being cut up on 18th December 1967. Photogrpah Peter Rose.

Standing with a single tank wagon on what was once the Down Withernsea line is Brush Type 4 diesel No.47349. This is the site of the one–time Joint Dock Junction, first brought into use during 1903 to allow construction trains access to the new dock, via a single track branch. An additional signal box was provided, and at the same time this part of the Withernsea branch was converted to double track. Some ten years later, in readiness for the opening of the new King George Dock, these lines were given over entirely to goods traffic. It would appear that the signal box then fell into disuse for a number of years. New passenger lines were constructed some yards to the north and the now long out of use brick arch of this diversion can be seen behind the engine in this 1988 view. Timber stacking grounds were eventually established in the area, and on 25th August 1920 a new interlocking frame of 30 levers was ordered. This was of the usual McKenzie & Holland No 16 type, but owing to changes in the structure of the signalling manufacturing industry was actually supplied by the Westinghouse Brake & Saxby Signal Co, works No.9254. By the early 1920s the signal box must have been back in use, and it reappears in the NER appendix of March 1st 1922, but now renamed Holderness Drain North. By the mid–1960s the movement of timber by rail was in rapid decline, and during 1967 the connections to two of the stacking grounds were removed. The end eventually came in February 1968 when the surviving timber sidings were dispensed with. Today this remaining single line forms the only rail link with both King George Dock and Saltend. It will ultimately join the former H&B route at Bridges Junction, reinstated in October 1968 for this very purpose. Photograph Steve Bramley.

Holderness Drain North July 1963. By the early 1920s much of this area was given over to timber storage, and three stacking grounds were soon established, designated A, B, and C plot. Prominent is A plot, sited more or less on the formation of the original Withernsea branch. B plot is to the right, access being via the trailing points in front of the signal box. The remaining group of sidings, C plot, lays between the goods lines and the Withernsea branch. These are to the west of the Holderness Drain, and thus not apparent in this scene. The signalling is a mixture of the old and the new, and although upper quadrant arms now predominate the miniature arm to C plot remains an original lower quadrant. Close study of the box reveals that at some time the end windows have been replaced, and they now have ten panes instead of the original eighteen. Despite its official title of many years standing, 'Holderness Drain North', the signal box name board reads only 'Holderness Drain'. At some time the down line span of the Drain bridge has been replaced, and although generally similar to the up line girders there are detail differences, the most notable being in the decking, and method of supporting the track. On the up line (to Hull, or the right hand span) the rails are supported on longitudinal waybeams, whilst on the down side (to King George dock) conventional sleepers are used. Photograph I.K. Watson.

A passenger train on the King George dock was most unusual, and apart from the Royal Train for the opening ceremony in June 1914 this may well have been the first. With the closure of the Hornsea and Withernsea branches imminent, on Saturday 10th October 1964 the West Riding Branch of the RCTS organised a tour of both the lines and the railways of Hull. The tour is seen on the Down H&BR goods line passing King George Dock signal box, heading in the Saltend direction. Although built by the Joint Dock committee the signal box and all signals were to the standard NER design. Above is the bridge carrying the high level coal lines to the berths and conveyors. Originally the signal box contained a frame of 90 levers of which Nos.61–90 were never used. These, as part of the great scrap drive of the last war, were eventually removed, probably on 10th November 1941. Both the high and low level lines were worked from the one signal box, which actually faced towards Hedon Road, so here we are looking at the rear. All the low level connections were concentrated between the first 20 levers. The wooden staging behind the box was provided to lead away and bring down to ground level all of the rodding and wire runss. When first opened in 1914 three signalmen were appointed, one for each shift, and paid £1.5s.0d each per 48 hour week. The signal (Down HB Goods Home Lever No.2) is a standard 22′ 6″ tubular post upper quadrant, which had replaced the original NER design some four years previously. Photograph John Foreman.

An interesting alternative use for a railway style semaphore signal, here controlling shipping into the lock entrance at the King George Dock, 7th June 1961. Lattice post signals were almost unknown in this area and we are unable to say with any certainty who would be responsible for its manufacture. The finial is a product of McKenzie & Holland. Unlike the conventional railway signals, the arm is not slotted through the post, and the lamp and spectacle also differ. The signal was worked by an electric motor located behind the arm Photograph Peter Rose.

SPRINGBANK WEST & SPRINGHEAD

Friday 18th September 1964. After shunting Calvert Lane coal depot 61032 STEMBOK heads towards Springbank South and eventually Empty Mineral Yard. The train is trip No.J11, a mid–morning pilot which first worked to Burleigh Street sidings and back, followed by two journeys to Springhead, the first with the wagon works traffic, and later with retail coal. No.11 water column stands isolated from the rest of the railway, its track having been lifted on the previous New Years Day; a reminder that 30 years ago the first day of the year was an ordinary working day. Photograph Peter Rose.

1963 and B1 61303 is crossing over Calvert Lane bridge with a short load of mineral wagons. The trip, J07, is the return working from Little Weighton, which at this date was the surviving Western outpost of the former H&BR main line. Just over a year later, in July 1964, this traffic ceased and the line behind Locomotive Junction signal box was closed. Springbank West signal box is visible in the middle distance, and was the last signal box to be built by the H&BR. This was a replacement for the original of 1885, and though sanctioned on the 29th November 1921, it was early LNER days before it was brought into use, at 5.00 a.m. on 5th February 1923. The contract price for the building was £537.18s.0d, the work to be completed within eight weeks. It is not recorded why there was a delay of some 15 months, but Messrs. Quibell, a local firm, were the contractors, and are still in business. The signal box remained gas lit until closure, which came at 4.45 p.m. on Saturday 7th November 1964. Springhead remained in use as a land sale coal depot until December 1989, when the railway connection was severed and lifted. The couple of remaining sidings, just off picture to the left of this yard, were known as 'New Marshalling', and eventually comprised 18 sidings. Not all of them were devoted to land sale coal. The train is on the Down Goods heading for Springbank South, 629 yards from West box. Behind are the now rarely used Up and Down branch lines to Springbank North (793 yards from West). Photograph Peter Rose.

Springhead shed about 1931. This view looking northwest from the Down main across the shed yard was probably taken on a Sunday. There's no sign of any activity, and all four engines are coaled up to capacity ready for their next call of duty. The leading engine did not enter LNER stock until January 1928, and had first been built for the Railway Operating Division as their No.1862 by the North British Locomotive Co. in April 1918. After nationalisation it eventually became BR No.63769, and remained in its original form until withdrawal during March 1959. Behind is an H&BR 0–6–0 still with its original domeless boiler, another R.O.D., and finally a further H&B type, now carrying a domed boiler. Across the shed yard is the front elevation of the 1908 coal stage. Centre of the picture are the former erecting shops and immediately adjoining, the engine shed.

Springhead engine shed from a similar vantage point but some years earlier about 1925 with H&BR 4–4–0s prominent in yet another seemingly empty yard.

WD 2–8–0 No.7071 at Springhead shed coupled to an ex–NER tender taken from Class C6 Atlantic No.532. This engine was built new in 1943 by Vulcan Foundry and after war service on the continent eventually became BR 90540. Though loaned to the LNER this engine, withdrawn July 1965, was never LNER property as were many others of the type. On 2nd December 1944 7071 was transferred to the Southern Railway and was observed at Eastleigh on 13th January 1945, still attached to its NER tender – painted khaki to match the locomotive. Two months later, on 11th March 1945, 7071 was shipped overseas, and four days after, it's former NER tender, No.8617, arrived back at Darlington.

Dignity and Impudence, together in Springhead shed yard, some time in the early 1930s. The larger of the two, is a Robinson 2–8–0, whilst Impudence takes the shape of former NER Class H 0–4–0T No.1799. Built at Gateshead works in March 1897, it was one of five transferred to the H&BR Section in 1922. These were all at Alexandra Dock shed, to replace the H&BR Kitson class K engines of the same wheel arrangement. Like their predecessors their sole duty was to shunt the quays. 1799 was transferred to Tyne Dock in 1935 remaining until withdrawn in 1946. During the Great War 1799 'joined the colours', and for a time served the Admiralty at Kyle of Lochalsh. Sister engine No.1798, which also came to Alexandra Dock in 1922, had an interesting career. It was loaned out to local industry on at least three occasions, in April/May 1925 it was at the Ideal Standard works, or as it was then called, the National Radiator Co. In September of the same year it could be found at the Melton works of Earle's cement. Six months later she was again away from home when during the February 1926 the British Extracting Co. hired it, to shunt their Hull depot.

D20 No.2022 and ex-GNR C12 No.4546 share part of the erecting shop in the 1930s. By 1935 no less than 16 of the latter type were resident in Hull.

Two scenes in the erecting shop in LNER days with H&BR locos dominant.

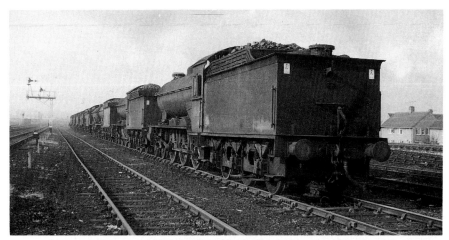

Probably never realising its full capacity, as main works and engine shed, during the latter LNER and BR periods, Springhead often played host to stored locomotives as these three photographs testify. Top to bottom B16's in 1960, D49's 1960, and J23's in 1934.

Like many other concerns during the Great War, the H&BR employed women. This group of cleaners give some scale to the 0–8–0.

Springhead engine shed being demolished, 16th October 1960. A line of stored B16/1s were at the top end of the yard and included 61436, 61443, 61413, 61422, 61416, 61425, 61423, 61419 and 61450. Photograph M. Lake.

During the mid–1950s half of Springhead engine shed was rebuilt in a style popular at the time, the remaining portion left open to the elements until closure in 1959. Diesel multiple units began to use the shed whilst Botanic Gardens was being refurbished and made ready to maintain all future dmu requirements in Hull.

Springhead 3rd July 1964, looking west across the former main line and overgrown engine yard, we have on the left the 185 foot long elevated coal stage, brought into use July 1908. Based on contemporary Great Northern Railway practice it was very similar to the New England stage – not surprising as the locomotive superintendent Matthew Stirling, was GN–trained, coming to Hull from New England. To the centre are the former locomotive erecting shops and to their right is the site of the now demolished engine shed. At the time of grouping 122 locomotives were allocated here. By now the entire site was devoted to wagon repair, carriage repairs having been moved to York as long ago as 1922. A 204 hp diesel mechanical shunter is setting a load of 'shops' into No.4 Reception Line. The two lines directly in front of the train are the Up and Down Goods to Springbank West box 1,246 yards away. Just visible, but much overgrown in the gap between the coal stage and erecting shops, are three long sidings. Of these the centre one served the turntable, long out of use but then still intact, whilst the right hand one served the connection to the Waterworks Tramway. The wagon works remained in use until 1971. Today most of the site has been given over to housing development, or lies vacant.

Passing Locomotive Junction signal box with return coal empties from Little Weighton and Willerby and Kirkella in September 1963 is B1 61255. It had been eight years since the passenger service to South Howden had ceased, and almost five years after the H&B was closed as a through line. Yet, quite astonishingly, by the standards of today all the signals and connections here were still retained in full working order. The former main lines, which effectively separated Springhead shed and works to the north from the sidings and marshalling yards to the south, are just visible between the engine and the rail built stop block. The signal, which is the Up Goods home (lever No.8), is worthy of a few lines. Some three years before this view, the powers that be had decided it was due for renewal. A photograph dated 16th October 1960 exists showing the new replacement erected a few yards in front, complete, but for some unknown reason this was not followed through, and it was subsequently taken away. The old signal then remained in use until the line closed, close observation showing the post has been strengthened from ground level. Another detail is the worn state of the arm, which now travels behind the usual 'ON' position. Fixed to the post just above the strengthening timbers is a cast plate, bearing the figure 8 lever number. This differs from the usual practice of screwing on individual numbers.

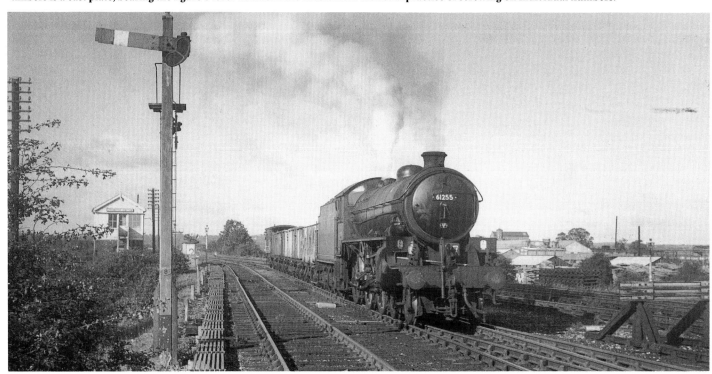

Organised chaos at Riverside Quay 9th June 1961, as the Danish bacon boat discharges through the transit shed (left). The covered vans at the platform formed the 5.50 pm Albert Dock – Manchester Oldham Road bacon train. To the right is the Albert Dock. In this area of the docks railway wagons were moved by shunt tractors, rather than locomotives; one can be seen near the police constable, while another one is moving a wagon beneath the first crane at Albert Dock. This scene was captured in the days when we had "...never had it so good". We were importing foodstuffs but virtually everything else on the dockside was for export. The heavy goods vehicles in view were all of British manufacture from household names such as Albion, Bedford, Commer, ERF, Fordson, Guy, Leyland, Morris most of which, thirty years on, do not exist.

Close to the 1840 terminus of the Hull and Selby Railway on 13th November 1963, with steam to spare, ex–Ministry of Supply saddle tank 68042 shunts out from under the Manor House yard gantry crane. Behind the engine the first wagon is an unfitted Boplate E whilst second and third are fitted and unfitted tube wagons. On the loading area are two Scammell trailers waiting their mechanical horses and the next call of duty.

It has not been possible to identify the work No.10 Pilot performed on 15th May 1959 when this picture was taken at Albert Dock. 68264 was a member of class J71, and was just eight months short of her 70th birthday when withdrawn in January 1960. As usual the front framing carries a couple of shunting poles, and also for good measure a spare tail lamp. The boiler hand rail has old rope and borrowed wagon sheet ties, used for securing the driver and firemans' push bikes.

On Saturday 26 July 1963 WD 2–8–0 No.90099 makes a smoky start as it heads past Neptune Street signal box bound for Withernsea. The train consists of one BR standard van and a brake. Even though both are fitted with the continuous brake, the engine headlight and the guards van sidelights indicate J05 is running loose coupled. The vehicle to the right of the train is loaded with an 'A' type container. Photograph Peter Rose.

Round timber on bolster wagons is included in the load of J05 pilot, 90272, as it makes its way off William Wright Dock. To the left, the trawler KINGSTON ONYX is in dry dock, with an unidentified tug in the next one. 22nd July 1963. Photograph Peter Rose.

Although in the main a picture of brick walls, this print tries to show something of the amount of activity carried on around the docks at the time. The principal performer is WD 90704 on pilot J05, having 'stopped the job' at the road roundabout between William Wright and St.Andrews Docks while propelling a load of vans towards William Wright Dock. A lorry which has emerged from the road subway between the two walls waits to continue left to William Wright Dock. Just beyond it the crossing attendant's cabin has a large bell, so that he can be summoned from outside by the Albert Dock signalman. The wires to the two shunt signals pass along the nearer wall. Behind the signals a water crane can be glimpsed. All around, large signs proclaim various dock related businesses. Date – 24th April 1964.

This is the view eastwards from Albert Dock box on 10th September 1963 as 61274, moves out of Exchange Sidings on a load for Empty Mineral Yard. The first part of the J07 diagram was to take any traffic from Inward Yard to Messrs. Ideal Standard's private sidings at Cottingham South Junction. After this it was to shunt Cottingham, and then return to Inward Yard via 7 Section. To complete the diagram the engine and men then worked to Control orders. Prior to the Hessle Road resignalling the Exchange sidings had been in constant use transferring traffic between the HB and NE Sections. The former H&BR is on the extreme left. Photograph Peter Rose.

In the mid–1930s the LNER invested heavily in this vicinity, generally simplifying the track layout and rationalizing the signalling. This culminated in the opening of the new Albert Dock signal box over the last weekend of January 1938. At the same time the old Albert Dock East box, which itself had taken over the work of Albert Dock West box from 1st March 1937, was closed, as was the H&B Subway box. Originally the transfer of traffic between the two systems H&B/NER, was almost nil. There was a through siding, but this was gated and securely locked, and the key, according to local folklore, could never be found. With the coming of the Joint Dock the two companies at last formed a working agreement. Then in 1914, ready for the opening of King George Dock, a proper junction was laid in at Liverpool Street to connect the H&BR with the NER No.4 box. Apart from the post–war reconstruction of Riverside Quay which was only temporary, and in any case built from recovered materials, Albert Dock was the last entirely new mechanical signal box to be erected within the city. Indeed there was no other new construction until late 1961 when work commenced on the present Hessle Road signal box. Owing to the effects of the Great War, Liverpool Street signal box was never put to proper use, and was eventually 'temporarily' closed for the duration. Later it was opened as and when required, and in later years at least was worked by the Subway signalman, who, when the need arose, travelled up on the pilot engine, transferred the train to the NE system, and then walked back to his own post. At 3.10 pm on 15th October 1926 the Liverpool Street box caught fire and that was the end of that. About 1928 a proper connection was once more established between the two systems. This time it was between the Subway box of the former H&B and Albert Dock East box NE Section. It was these 1928 connections which formed the basis of the Exchange Sidings incorporated into the 1938 Albert Dock box. To most local railwaymen it was never referred to by its proper name – just the simple 'Exchange'.

Looking westwards to Albert Dock box, the predominant feature is footbridge No.5. Although not evident, the bridge is out of use and will be removed on Sunday 26th April 1964, two days after this record. The connections at left are to Found Out Sidings. On the right are the chimneys of four fish curing factories, once a prominent sight on the old Hessle Road skyline. In these the herrings were hung and smoked to be turned into kippers. Up to the time of this picture practically everyone who lived along or near Hessle Road owed their living to the fishing industry.

O4 2–8–0 No.63913 of Staveley G.C. shed comes up from Albert Dock Exchange Sidings with a load for Outward Yard. 14th August 1963. Photograph Peter Rose.

At St Andrews Dock on 27th October 1961, and under the watchful eye of two members of the local railway police, 69011 gets about the business of making up a fish train. Here, instead of the usual cobbles, the track is neatly filled with concrete, including a double slip alongside the engine. Meanwhile on the footplate, to protect themselves from the Humber 'Breeze', the crew have rigged up a rudimentary storm sheet, no doubt 'borrowed' from any convenient wagon. Photograph Peter Rose.

A very grimy and unidentified J25 gets about the business of setting up a train of fish empties at the Fish Dock in 1960. All track and pointwork is laid into stone sets including, under the engine, a double slip. Note also the special arrangement of the point hand levers.

St Andrews Dock signal box seen from the east in October 1964. Behind on the embankment are the main passenger lines which are still in use today. The remaining goods lines were swept away in the late 1960s, and are now the site of Clive Sullivan Way. Photograph Ian K Watson.

We suspect that this picture, taken in July 1954 not far from St Andrews Dock signal box, (probably on No.2 West Reception Line) was a posed publicity shot. The 350 HP diesel shunter No.13077 is in a very clean if not pristine condition as are the wagons with their block load of export tractors. These will eventually be tripped across the city for shipment.

B1 61080 came off the road in Found Out Sidings, Albert Dock, and had to be lifted a fair height in order to set the bogie wheels back on top of the rails – date of picture is 26th March 1963. J07 worked traffic from Inward Yard to the Ideal Boilers & Radiators works, Cottingham and Waterworks coal (at Cottingham), and shunted 7 Section, Inward Yard and Loaded Tanks, going then to Dairycoates shed for Control Orders. 61080 is 'Engine & Van' working 'to Control Orders'. As always the incident had attracted the usual group of onlookers, all no doubt forthcoming with the necessary advice as to how the job should be carried out. Photograph Peter Rose.

Although serious accidents were fortunately few and far between, minor mishaps and derailments were a common occurrence in a busy shunting yard. At 6.30 pm on 25th July 1963 Esso tank No.3655 appears to have split a pair of points just below the hump at the east end of Outward Yard. The tank had come from Saltend and was destined to be worked on to Horncastle in Lincolnshire. Within 15 minutes of the derailment the Dairycoates breakdown crane was on hand and ready to start the rerailing process. 1½ hours later all was in order, and the crane was away back to shed by 9.00 pm. Photograph Peter Rose.

Recorded from the steps of St.Andrews Dock box, 90272 on J01 pilot bustles along with Presflo cement wagons. Just right of the engine smokebox are the Outward Yard Reception lines, with the engine release line coming past the signal. 23rd June 1964. Photograph Peter Rose.

Looking eastwards across Outward Yard from the top of a lighting tower on 4th September 1965. The girders of 5A bridge taking the passenger lines over the goods lines at Dairycoates West are on the extreme left. Behind are the water tower and coaling plant of Dairycoates shed and, on the extreme right, the River Humber and the 'fish dock'. Amongst the general mix of rolling stock prominent in the foreground with their peaked roofs are five continental ferry vans. Photograph Peter Rose.

Outward Yard seen from the west. In the yard B1 61012 PUKU prepares to depart with the 7.35 p.m. Washwood Heath fully fitted freight. 2nd May 1963. Photograph Peter Rose.

Although carrying a 50E Scarborough shedplate, BR Standard 3MT 2–6–0 77004 was, in 1963, working from Dairycoates shed. On 5th March it has detached freight traffic off J19 pilot at Outward Yard, and is setting off with hoppers to cross the main lines at Hessle East, en route to Empty Mineral Yard.

The fireman of B1 61179 puts up fully fitted headlamps before working the 4.10 p.m. London fish on 2nd March, 1963. From May that year, the job was diagrammed to a Dairycoates B1.

HESSLE HAVEN & INWARD YARD

Looking east down the hump of the New Inward yard. Complete closure took place in March 1974. Photograph N.E. Stead

(opposite top) The fully fitted London fish train, with Kings Cross B1 61393 on the front, waits impatiently for the road alongside Hessle Haven signal box in June 1964. Although strictly outside the city boundary, this is where the Hull railway system begins. Behind the camera are the junctions which lead to the Inward, and Loaded Mineral yards. Apart from the recently erected colour light signal, out of use behind the engine, this scene is almost timeless and little altered from when the signal box opened some 50 odd years previously. This was all soon to change, and within months the Down Slow, the line nearest the signal box, would be taken out of use. From now on it was all downhill – even so decline was to take a further 19 years. The end finally came in the early hours of Sunday 27th February 1983 when, at 3.34 am, Hessle Haven box closed for ever. As late as 17th July 1975 a level crossing was brought into use more or less on the site where the engine stands. By that time the Up and Down Slow lines had long been lifted. The crossing had lifting barriers, but was worked mechanically from the signal box by a gate wheel. After much research it is concluded that this was probably the last such new installation in the country; put in as part of the Humber Bridge project, much of the steel fabrication work was done in what had been Priory Yard. With the abolition of the signal box the level crossing was also abandoned. Photograph Peter Rose.

(opposite bottom) Hessle Haven looking west. On the left, complete with its own siding, is Hessle Gas works, referred to on some plans as 'Gashouse'. From left to right the lines are Up Goods, Up Main, Down Fast, Down Slow. The train is running onto the Down North Goods, crossing both Down lines and connected to the Up Fast is the Up South Goods line. Behind are the 'North and South Inward' lines to the new Inward Yard. The facing trap marks the point where the Up Goods becomes the Up Slow line. Picture taken from the Up Slow/Main signal gantry by Peter Rose.

An elevated view eastwards from the hump top at Inward Yard West showing, left to right: two engine release lines; two shunt necks for the Secondary Sorting Sidings; Primary Sorting Sidings numbers 1–30, with the four retarders at the entrance to each group; the Control Tower; No.1 Down North Main line; Up North Main Line. 22nd January 1963. Photograph Peter Rose.

Double heading was uncommon in the Hull area. There was at one time an oil train from Saltend to Neville Hill diagrammed to double headed WDs – and what a sight that must have been, ascending the bank to Garforth (unfortunately during the night, therefore no photographs). Here 90435 and 90351 are nearing Loaded Mineral Yard with an incoming train. In the right background are wagons standing on Inward Yard Receptions. A few years later there was an almost daily double headed turn worked by Dairycoates men and engines. This was from Saltend to the West Riding via the Victoria Dock branch; on many occasions this would be two WDs, but occasionally a WD and a B1 could be seen. Once, towards the end of steam working, this turn was triple headed, by two Paxman Type 1 0–6–0 diesels and a WD. 22nd January 1963.

Inward Yard east end, looking west towards the hump with the control tower prominent. The nearer diesel shunter, D3675, was built at Darlington, emerging June 1958 and sent new to Springhead; always a Hull engine, it was withdrawn from Botanic Gardens as 08513 in March 1978 and cut up at Doncaster Works during the following October. The other diesel, BR built to an LMS 1945 design, carries a number in the 12113 – 12119 range – unfortunately the last digit is mostly obscured by a handrail but is is possibly 4. B1 61176 is making up a train out of No.17 road, and will have to collect a brakevan. What cannot be seen, even with careful scanning through a glass, are the wheel skates which in this yard were used to bring to a stand the first wagon into a siding, to prevent it from running out of the east end of the yard. Other points worth a mention – compared with the modern railway, how relatively clean and tidy the whole area appears; Anlaby Park flats under construction in the background; all point hand levers painted white for night working. Photograph Peter Rose.

This 18th January, 1962 view from the main line overbridge shows the layout at the south side of Dairycoates West Junction before the rationalisation concurrent with the opening of the North Goods lines and Hessle Road flyover. The points in the right hand pair of lines have already been clamped towards St.Andrews Dock box, and the signal arm for Inward and Mineral Yards has been removed. WD 90006 uses the remaining access lines toward Inward and Mineral Yards. Note the shrubs planted on the right and their little concrete borders – the idea of John Miller, the LNER's one–time civil engineer. There are also PW men about – their shovels can be seen laid in the 4ft. and 6ft. on the St Andrews Dock lines. Photograph Peter Rose.

Looking west, 14th September 1965. A bird's eye view of Dairycoates West Jct, taken from the top of the coaling plant. The two lines on the left, complete with scissors crossover, lead to the engine shed. A group of platelayers are busy packing the Up South branch and behind them are the connections to 7 section, which by now was already becoming the storage ground for scrap locos. On the embankment are the Up and Down Main or Selby lines over which Dairycoates West signalbox had no control. Behind the embankment can be made out the form of the North branch and other connections laid new in early 1962 as part of the Hessle Road resignalling. Photograph Peter Rose.

Class 01 No.63646 of 41H (Staveley GC shed) has obviously been borrowed by Dairycoates shed. Seen here coming from Inward Yard, and joining the North Branch with J19 Pilot it is probably en route for Wilmington goods yard, via the Victoria Dock branch. Prior to 1915 and the building of 5A Bridge and the embankments, the main passenger lines were more or less on the site of the North Branch.

67684 with one of the inward workings from Brough, on the Down Main passing over the Hull Central goods lines at Dairycoates West Junction, 2nd March 1963.

Winter decorations in 7 Section Sidings, Dairycoates. 67677; 61952; 64850; 61969; 61906; 61819; and 61930 share the chill, 25th February, 1963.

A 10.00 a.m. special freight of about 25 sheeted highbar wagons, destined for York via Market Weighton, heads past Dairycoates West in the charge of 90695, 16th April 1963. Notice the simplified track layout as compared to earlier pictures, also colour light signal with route indication instead of semaphore signals. The train is coming off the Down St Andrews Dock branch crossing the Up & Down Mains and is about to join the Down South Branch.

69009 passes Dairycoates West box in January 1962, with Driver Tommy Atkinson on the footplate. Note both 7 and 62 pilot numbers chalked on the bunker of the J72. From about 1957 both pilot duties were designated for 350 h.p. diesel shunters – '7 Pilot was Inward Yard – two trips Inward Yard to Manor House, breakfast; Belle Vue to Inward Yard 12.30 p.m. trip Inward Yard to Manor House; Works 6.30 p.m. trip Manor House to Outward Yard; Shunt and Trips as Required. 62 Pilot shunts Neptune Street (H&B)'. Photograph Peter Rose.

Seen here on 1st June 1965, from Dairycoates West signal box, WD Austerity No.90008 with its load of one empty mineral wagon runs tender first off the Up South branch. Meanwhile a group of platelayers stand back interrupted from their work of levelling and packing the Junction. The man with the jacket will be the Ganger in charge of the four platelayers. As a clue to the work about to be done he holds in his right hand a 'levelling board'. 90008 had for many years been a Hull engine, and appropriately enough ended her days here when she was cut up by Drapers on 26th June 1967. In all, 201 examples of the 733 BR WD 2–8–0s were cut up locally, the first being No.90602 on 22nd March 1965 and the last Nos.90611 and 90642 on 6th May 1968. Photograph Peter Rose.

Looking north east from the coaling plant 14th September 1965, with a Birmingham RC&W Class 104 dmu forming the 11.05 am Sheffield service passing 7 Section. A variety of coaching stock awaits its next call of duty, including a stranger in the camp in the form of an unidentified former Great Western coach. There are nine locomotives ready for their final journey to Drapers Sculcoates yard, from left to right 63590, 63646, 42477, 44386, 42109, 63879, 44587, 44277, and 92195, none of them Dairycoates engines. In the middle distance can be seen the road flyover, then two years old, and Hessle Road signal box. Photograph Peter Rose.

Shunting out under 5A bridge is 350 hp diesel shunter No.13081; later it would become D3081 and eventually, under 'TOPS', 08066. The short train of eight covered vans contains an interesting mix of vehicles – apart from the BR period, all four of the former companies are represented. Being merely a shunting move confined to yard working, the train is by 'special authority' and exempt from the requirement to have a brake van. Table H1 of the *Sectional Appendix* refers to the circumstances in which freight vehicles could be worked without a brake van in the rear: *One wagon of coal or stores for signal boxes and stations, or empty wagon in connection there with, may be worked without a brake van between any two signal boxes, provided the signal boxes concerned are not more than one mile apart. In all cases where fitted vehicles are authorised to be worked without a brake van in rear, the automatic brake must be connected up and in use.* At about the time of this picture there were 26 locations within the city where this form of working was permitted. Six of these were authorised here at Dairycoates West: to and from St Andrews Dock – Hessle Road – Dairycoates East. Here 7 Pilot is drawing off the Down North No.1 Mineral line and under the authority of Dairycoates West No.86 signal is bound towards Dairycoates East box via the Down North Main. The signal bracket is typical of the middle period of LNER practice. This example will have been erected in the mid 1930s, when in connection with the opening of the new Inward yard extensive alterations were carried out. 7 Pilot was provided by Dairycoates, and as early as 1957 was booked for a diesel. It was stationed at Inward Yard and among its booked jobs was to trip to Manor House, the train seen in this picture. All fitted vans, its make up is LNER, BR, GW, BR, LNER, BR, LMS, and finally (given away by its roof contour) a former Southern Railway type. No.13081 is well adorned with shunt sticks – two poked into the leading steps, and another wedged behind the No 7 trip board. The building visible in the middle background is home to the products of the world famous Mr Birdseye.

Staveley O1 No.63590 has been borrowed between turns by Dairycoates on 10th September 1963, and is here leaving 7 Section heading towards Dairycoates West. The view shows to advantage the great bulk of the 'coal cracker', and how the coal was elevated up from ground level to the storage bunkers. Engines were served from both sides and in this picture what appears to be a V1 or V3 tank is being coaled from the east side shute. Photograph Peter Rose.

The rebuilding of the vast Dairycoates engine shed required that four of the old NER roundhouses be taken down for a new twin turntable shed to be fashioned from the remaining roundhouses. This view inside the shed in January 1957 gives some idea of the pitched roof design of the old sheds.

Some nine months later the new concrete and steel frame of the shed is taking shape around the original turntables and engine pits. Provision to alter the track layout to a straight road scheme was made with future main line diesel locomotive maintenance requirements in mind.

By December 1957 the shed was taking shape. All the while locomotives continued to shelter where they could.

It is now April 1967, and the end of steam is only weeks away as WD 2–8–0s Nos.90450, 90478 and 90272, all in steam, stand round the turntable in Dairycoates shed. 90450 was withdrawn from Dairycoates in June and eventually cut up by Drapers in their Neptune Street yard on 8th January 1968. 90478 was no stranger to the area and had been a Springhead engine for many years. When steam ended at 50B it was moved away to West Hartlepool where it remained in service until September. On the right are four ex–Western Region Paxman engined Type 1 0–6–0 diesels, short lived interim replacements for steam traction. Only three of these are identified – D9510, D9525 and D9547. Photograph Peter Rose.

B16/3 61472 stands in Dairycoates roundhouse awaiting its next turn of duty, on 27th March 1963. Despite outshopping from Darlington only 12 days previously, only a year or so later – on 20th April 1964, it was condemned. After being dumped 61472 was sold in September that year and made its final journey to Messrs. Drapers, Sculcoates scrapyard for cutting up on 9th November. In all nine members of Class B16 were scrapped by Drapers including 61420, which was the first steam locomotive to be dealt with by them. Photograph Peter Rose.

Dairycoates 27th September 1958. When this view was captured, 62700 YORKSHIRE, a one time Botanic engine, would never steam again. Stood alongside but very much alive, 43077 is ready for work. A few days later the D49 would be officially condemned, its LMS–designed stablemate was however destined to survive well into the next decade, and was finally cut up locally by Drapers on 28th August 1967. Of modelling interest is the permanent way, laid over the inspection pits with conventional chairs and bullhead rail. This of course is quite the opposite from the picture inside Springhead shed seen elsewhere.

Class 01 63795 being coaled at the Dairycoates coal hopper on 8th May, 1963. As No.6595, this was the first engine to be rebuilt from Class 04, in February 1944. Photograph Peter Rose.

9Fs were a rare sight, but did turn up from time to time. 92010 is heading for Dairycoates shed after working in a train of motor vehicles, when caught by the cameraman on 9th June 1964. At this time it was allocated to 9D Newton Heath, suggesting the cars were the product of the Ford Halewood factory. These would almost certainly be for export, and would later be tripped to King George Dock for eventual shipment overseas. Photograph Peter Rose.

In the preparation of this volume the authors called upon the help and co-operation of numerous individuals and groups. Amongst those who contributed documents, photographs and encouragement we give an especial thanks to Michael Back, Steve Bramley, John Dixon, Nick Fleetwood, John Francis, Steve Jordan, Mike Lake, Roy Richardson, Peter Rose and Ian K. Watson. Also thanks to the many railwaymen past and present, whose local knowledge brought out some overlooked facts from the past. To be placed on record by one of the authors is a debt of gratitude to the late J.B. Stork, who passed on the importance of research if any history is to be considered worthy. Thanks also to the North Eastern Railway Association and the Signalling Record Society. If we have left any person out of this acknowledgement we apologise for the omission. Finally, many thanks to Ida and Annie for putting up with it all so gracefully. M.N. and W.B.Y. Hull 1993.